W9-BCB-309

NEW DIRECTIONS FOR INSTITUTIONAL RESEARCH

Patrick T. Terenzini, *The Pennsylvania State University*
EDITOR-IN-CHIEF

Using Performance Indicators to Guide Strategic Decision Making

Victor M. H. Borden
Indiana University–Purdue University Indianapolis

Trudy W. Banta
Indiana University–Purdue University Indianapolis

EDITORS

NUMBER 82, SUMMER 1994

JOSSEY-BASS PUBLISHERS
San Francisco

USING PERFORMANCE INDICATORS
TO GUIDE STRATEGIC DECISION MAKING
Victor M. H. Borden, Trudy W. Banta (eds.)
New Directions for Institutional Research, no. 82
Volume XVI, Number 2
Patrick T. Terenzini, Editor-in-Chief

© 1994 by Jossey-Bass Inc., Publishers. All rights reserved.

No part of this issue may be reproduced in any form—except for a brief
quotation (not to exceed 500 words) in a review or professional work—
without permission in writing from the publishers.

Microfilm copies of issues and articles are available in 16mm and 35mm,
as well as microfiche in 105mm, through University Microfilms Inc., 300
North Zeeb Road, Ann Arbor, Michigan 48106-1346.

LC 85-645339   ISSN 0271-0579   ISBN 0-7879-9964-4

NEW DIRECTIONS FOR INSTITUTIONAL RESEARCH is part of The Jossey-Bass
Higher and Adult Education Series and is published quarterly by Jossey-
Bass Inc., Publishers, 350 Sansome Street, San Francisco, California
94104-1342 (publication number USPS 098-830). Second-class postage
paid at San Francisco, California, and at additional mailing offices. POST-
MASTER: Send address changes to New Directions for Institutional
Research, Jossey-Bass Inc., Publishers, 350 Sansome Street, San Francisco,
California 94104-1342.

SUBSCRIPTIONS for 1994 cost $47.00 for individuals and $62.00 for institutions, agencies, and libraries.

EDITORIAL CORRESPONDENCE should be sent to the Editor-in-Chief, Patrick
T. Terenzini, Center for the Study of Higher Education, The Pennsylvania
State University, 403 South Allen Street, Suite 104, University Park,
Pennsylvania 16801-5202.

Photograph of the library by Michael Graves at San Juan Capistrano by
Chad Slattery © 1984. All rights reserved.

Manufactured in the United States of America. Nearly all Jossey-Bass
books, jackets, and periodicals are printed on recycled paper that contains
at least 50 percent recycled waste, including 10 percent postconsumer
waste. Many of our materials are also printed with vegetable-based inks;
during the printing process, these inks emit fewer volatile organic com-
pounds (VOCs) than petroleum-based inks. VOCs contribute to the for-
mation of smog.

THE ASSOCIATION FOR INSTITUTIONAL RESEARCH was created in 1966 to benefit, assist, and advance research leading to improved understanding, planning, and operation of institutions of higher education. Publication policy is set by its Publications Board.

PUBLICATIONS BOARD

Timothy R. Sanford (Chair)	University of North Carolina, Chapel Hill
Louis C. Attinasi, Jr.	University of Houston, University Park
Charles H. Belanger	Laurentian University
Mary K. Kinnick	Portland State University
Marsha V. Krotseng	State College and University Systems of West Virginia
J. Fredericks Volkwein	State University of New York at Albany

EX-OFFICIO MEMBERS OF THE PUBLICATIONS BOARD

Jean J. Endo	University of Colorado, Boulder
John A. Lucas	William Rainey Harper College
Larry W. Nelson	Pacific Lutheran University
John C. Smart	University of Illinois–Chicago
Patrick T. Terenzini	The Pennsylvania State University

For information about the Association for Institutional Research, write to the following address:

AIR Executive Office
314 Stone Building
Florida State University
Tallahassee, Florida 32306-3038

(904) 644-4470

CONTENTS

EDITORS' NOTES   1
Victor M. H. Borden, Trudy W. Banta

1. Performance Indicators: History, Definitions, and Methods   5
Victor M. H. Borden, Karen V. Bottrill
This history of performance indicators in the United States and Europe
is developed as a context for understanding the definitions and the methods used to develop them.

2. Data, Indicators, and the National Center for Higher Education   23
Management Systems
Peter T. Ewell, Dennis P. Jones
Indicator development is conceptualized as part of a broader approach
to management information and decision making.

3. Performance Indicators and Quality Assessment in European   37
Higher Education
Ben W. A. Jongbloed, Don F. Westerheijden
The historical development of performance indicators in the countries of
the European Community provides a backdrop for consideration of the
quality assurance methods being proposed in Europe today.

4. Total Quality Management Perspective on Assessing   51
Institutional Performance
Michael J. Dooris, Deborah J. Teeter
TQM methods yield indicators that can be used to monitor and improve
the quality and effectiveness of implementation processes in colleges and
universities.

5. Using Key Performance Indicators to Drive Strategic   63
Decision Making
Michael G. Dolence, Donald M. Norris
The Strategic Decision Engine is a nine-step method for defining and
pursuing performance indicators derived from a strategic planning
process.

6. Activity-Based Costing Model for Assessing   81
Economic Performance
Daniel W. DeHayes, Joseph G. Lovrinic
An activity-based costing model yields information that can be used to
judge the value added by each component activity required to produce
an educational product such as classroom instruction.

7. Performance Indicators for Accountability and   95
Improvement
Trudy W. Banta, Victor M. H. Borden
The history, theory, and practice from preceding chapters are synthesized
in guidelines for institutional development of performance indicators.

8. Appendix: Examples from the Literature   107
Karen V. Bottrill, Victor M. H. Borden
More than 250 performance indicators are grouped in 22 categories
drawn from 14 references.

INDEX   121

Editors' Notes

Performance indicators have emerged in response to pressures for colleges and universities to demonstrate their value and effectiveness. These pressures are coming from a variety of sources, including national and state governments, boards of trustees, accrediting agencies, and students and their families. Although the call for accountability is nothing new to higher education, there seems to be an increasing number of vested parties, often with divergent interests, making increasingly sophisticated and intrusive attempts to monitor and influence the way colleges and universities operate.

Throughout the developed world, and especially in the United States, institutions of higher education have invested significant resources in demonstrating their effectiveness. Monthly meetings of boards of trustees, institution-wide strategic planning efforts, state-mandated student outcomes assessment initiatives, institutional self-study for re-accreditation, and academic program review are but a few of the types of performance appraisal to which institutions are subject. Yet despite all the efforts to comply with accountability demands, there is a widespread impression that, on the whole, higher education institutions have not yet succeeded in conveying their value and effectiveness to an increasingly skeptical public.

In this issue of *New Directions for Institutional Research*, we examine the international movement toward the development of performance indicator systems for accountability and improvement in higher education. Our goals are threefold: to provide the reader with an understanding of what has led to the current popularity of indicator systems; to illustrate several possible methods for developing performance indicators; and to synthesize theory and practice into a formulation for a proactive, institution-based approach to indicator development.

The volume begins with a general overview of performance indicators (PIs). In the first chapter, Victor Borden and Karen Bottrill describe the history of PIs in the United States and Europe as a context for understanding the definitions of PIs and the methods used to develop them. The authors describe the input–process–output framework that lies behind most approaches to higher education performance appraisal and show how this conceptualization helps to classify PI development efforts.

In Chapter Two, Peter Ewell and Dennis Jones continue in this broad-stroke manner to explore the development of PIs in the United States. They link this development with the quarter-century evolution of the National Center for Higher Education Management Systems (NCHEMS). Ewell and Jones provide recent examples of indicator systems from states and institutions in this country.

In Chapter Three, Ben Jongbloed and Don Westerheijden conduct a parallel analysis of European PI approaches over the last two decades. From their vantage point in the Center for Higher Education Policy Studies (CHEPS) in The Netherlands, these authors are particularly well-qualified to judge the commonalities and differences in PI development among the countries of the European Community. Jongbloed and Westerheijden explore the contemporary development of quality assurance methods in European higher education as a departure from prior government-initiated efforts that have produced the most comprehensive literature in the world on the subject of performance indicators.

Chapters Four through Six present more specific approaches to PI development. In Chapter Four, Michael Dooris and Deborah Teeter discuss PI development from a total quality management (TQM) perspective. Using examples from The Pennsylvania State University, the authors demonstrate how process-oriented TQM methods yield indicators that have direct consequences for monitoring and improving the quality and effectiveness of higher education operations.

In Chapter Five, Michael Dolence and Donald Norris describe a Strategic Decision Engine (SDE) model for using key performance indicators (KPIs) as the focal point for a strategic planning process. The SDE model is a nine-step cyclical method for defining and pursuing strategic objectives expressed through levels of performance on the KPIs. These authors use examples from the University of Northern Colorado and Illinois Benedictine College to illustrate how they have used the SDE framework in practice.

The last of the three methods chapters is contributed by Daniel DeHayes and Joseph Lovrinic. In it they describe an activity-based costing methodology that they have developed and applied successfully to several academic and administrative programs at Indiana University-Purdue University Indianapolis (IUPUI). Their economic model takes an endpoint-first engineering approach to costing the products of an educational or administrative program. The cost information is used to judge the value added to the product by each component activity required to produce that product. DeHayes and Lovrinic illustrate how one of Indiana University's professional schools used this information to restructure and reduce unnecessary administrative overhead.

In the final chapter of this issue, the editors synthesize the discussions of theory, history, and practice from the preceding chapters to provide a set of guidelines for the proactive development of performance indicators. We suggest that PI development is optimally initiated at the university- or college-wide level, but requires extensive coordination with academic and administrative units within the institution, as well as with governing and coordinating groups and with stakeholders outside the institution. Approached in this multitiered, multimethod, and coordinated fashion, PIs can provide an information-based approach to both accountability and improvement.

The appendix to this issue contains examples of more than 250 potential performance indicators grouped into 22 categories that were drawn from 14 listed references. Although these examples are by no means exhaustive of the possibilities, they illustrate the variety of forms that PIs may take.

Institutional researchers and others who supply information to support decision-making activities in higher education can play an important role in the development of performance indicators throughout the higher education sector. PIs represent a measurement-based approach to institutional performance appraisal that one can tie to program objectives and to the procedures for attaining those objectives. By working closely with program administrators and operations managers and by applying expertise in the areas of measurement and data analysis, the IR practitioner can serve as information broker in the development process. It is our hope that this issue of NDIR provides a context for understanding how best to deploy a PI development process as well as a sufficient number of concrete examples of methods and specific indicators to prepare readers to contribute to any such developmental effort within their own institution, system, or program.

Victor M. H. Borden
Trudy W. Banta
Editors

VICTOR M. H. BORDEN is director of information management and institutional research and assistant professor of psychology at Indiana University–Purdue University Indianapolis.

TRUDY W. BANTA is vice chancellor for planning and institutional improvement and professor of higher education at Indiana University–Purdue University Indianapolis.

With a long tacit history in the United States and a shorter but more explicit history in Europe, performance indicators have now come to the forefront as a strategic method for evaluating colleges and universities.

Performance Indicators: History, Definitions, and Methods

Victor M. H. Borden, Karen V. Bottrill

"Our mandate is clear. . . . We are going to have to prove that we deserve the dollars spent on higher education and justify our asking for each additional dollar" (p. 1). So begins *The Outputs of Higher Education: Their Identification, Measurement and Evaluation,* a report summarizing the proceedings of a seminar sponsored in 1970 by three organizations that were leading efforts to improve the management of colleges and universities: the Western Interstate Commission for Higher Education (WICHE), the American Council on Education (ACE), and the Center for Research and Development in Higher Education (CRDHE) at the University of California, Berkeley (Lawrence, Weathersby, and Patterson, 1970).

This quarter-century-old call to arms still resounds clearly today in higher education throughout the developed world. In response, there has been an outpouring of opinion and mandates to document more effectively the value and achievements of colleges and universities. National governments, state and provincial legislatures, boards of trustees, and professional accrediting agencies are calling for concrete evidence that institutions of higher education are worth the large public and private investments they receive. Ironically, representatives of these agencies are increasing their accountability demands at the same time that many are decreasing their investments. As the burden of increasing costs is shifting directly to the consumer of higher education services—present and potential students and their families, as well as business and industry—consumer interest in proof of the value of a college education is also mounting.

Performance indicators (PIs) have emerged largely in response to these pressures. The Organization for Economic Cooperation and Development

(OECD) (see Kells, 1993) and several other European research centers have made this concept a cornerstone of their work in higher education management. Although this terminology has only recently become popular here, in many ways PIs have a longer and more complex history of development in the United States.

Performance indicators represent a very simple and compelling idea. They are measures of how well something is being done. But beyond this simple definition lie many complicated issues regarding who defines the goals and criteria for performance, who uses these indicators and for what purposes, and the many technical issues that surround any measurement effort.

In this chapter, we first consider the historical and current contexts from which PIs have emerged. We then present some pertinent issues and concepts as a framework for defining and better understanding PIs. Finally, we discuss some of the practical aspects surrounding the development of PIs within higher education systems, institutions, and programs.

Historical Context: PIs in the United States

Research and practice in performance measurement of colleges and universities have long histories in the United States. Cave, Hanney, and Kogan (1991) trace these activities to college reputational ranking studies conducted as early as 1910. Institutional comparisons have long been the most common method for public assessment of quality. College guidebooks and national magazines have for many years produced annual listings of the top colleges and university programs according to a variety of criteria. In addition, peer comparisons have a long tradition within the higher education sector as a means of measuring progress and performance. The American Council on Education's ranking of doctoral programs (Roose and Anderson, 1970), the Carnegie classifications of all institutions (Carnegie Foundation for the Advancement of Teaching, 1987), and the Gourman Report rankings of graduate and undergraduate programs (Gourman, 1993a, 1993b) represent attempts to establish broad-based criteria for comparing colleges and universities and their programs.

Peer comparisons have been considered a valuable method for assessing some specific aspects of higher education, such as faculty workload and salary guidelines. As evidence of the importance institutional researchers have attached to peer comparisons, two earlier volumes of the *New Directions for Institutional Research* series (Peterson, 1976; Brinkman, 1987) have been devoted to explorations of these methods. A number of data-sharing consortia have developed among various types of higher education institutions to expedite the conduct of institutional comparisons. Acute interest in institutional comparisons continues today, as is evident in the recent book by Taylor, Meyerson, and Massy (1993), *Strategic Indicators for Higher Education: Improving Performance*. This volume presents a series of normative indicators on finance, facilities, academic operations, and student characteristics for use by higher education governing boards as measures of institutional performance.

Reputational rankings and other types of institutional comparisons have incorporated a wide variety of criteria and have been used for many different purposes. Jordan (1989) suggests that they have been influential but that the enormous range of criteria and uses contributes more to a mystique of gauging higher education program performance than to its serious appraisal.

Resource allocation measures emerged in the 1960s as another important component of higher education performance appraisal. During this period of vast expansion in the U.S. higher education sector, the focus of college and university management shifted toward the efficient management of resources—the fiscal, physical, and human inputs into the higher education enterprise. The work of the Western Interstate Council for Higher Education (WICHE) and its offshoot, the National Center for Higher Education Management Systems (NCHEMS), generated many useful methods and measures for making decisions about how to allocate the relatively plentiful resources of higher education. NCHEMS developed the Resource Requirements Prediction Model (RRPM) to assist college and university administrators in making decisions about funding priorities and levels of performance efficiency. This model made popular the measure of cost per student credit hour as the benchmark of institutional efficiency. A number of computer-based resource allocation and planning models were developed around the same time as RRPM, including CAMPUS, HIS, TUSS, HELP/PLANTRAN, and CAP:SC/SEARCH. Mason (1976) summarizes the availability, uses, benefits, and drawbacks of these computer modeling efforts.

The growth of U.S. higher education continued through the 1970s and 1980s as did the size of the public and private investment in the enterprise. Zemsky and Massy (1990) demonstrate how the growth in fiscal and workforce terms far exceeded growth in enrollments. Colleges and universities became very large and diversified businesses where faculty were increasingly specialized and research-oriented. At the same time, administrators developed professional components to support research, provide nonacademic support to students (such as health care), and take over some of the traditional duties of faculty, such as student advising.

Professionalization of the business side of higher education was promoted by the National Association for College and University Business Officers (NACUBO). Through publications, conferences, seminars, and workshops, NACUBO members have embraced various methods for supporting and evaluating the management of higher education institutions. This business orientation to higher education produced a greater interest in the economics of college and university operations. In his 1992 article in the *NACUBO Business Officer,* Turk describes activity-based costing methodologies for generating financial performance information as a basis for cost containment strategies.

In Chapter Six of this volume, Daniel DeHayes and Joseph Lovrinic describe a related method for monitoring the economic performance of higher education programs.

In 1991, NACUBO embarked on a project in cooperation with Coopers and Lybrand to collect more than 200 comparative measures of institutional operations from a wide range of colleges and universities (see Rush, 1994). These measures cover operations ranging from student admissions to the purchasing of office supplies. This effort, and others like it, have expanded the domain of institutional comparisons from an early focus on reputations to an emphasis on efficient use of resources.

The professionalization of higher education management was also promoted by the development of a strategic planning paradigm. George Keller's (1983) seminal work described some of the early efforts to bring a strategic business planner's orientation to the development of higher education institutions. His book stimulated the interest of many college and university leaders, especially a growing breed of entrepreneurial leaders. Robert Shirley's model (1982) furnished a framework for institutional planning efforts that became popular among planning professionals.

Strategic planning provides an up-front, information-based approach to institutional development. The method requires one to first state the purpose and goals of a college or university. Institutional leaders must then consider the feasibility of pursuing those goals within the current and future social and political environments and make strategic choices about how to proceed. In Chapter Five of this volume, Michael Dolence and Donald Norris illustrate the application of a strategic planning approach that is based on the articulation and monitoring of key performance indicators.

The strategic planning approach has proven successful in a variety of settings, but has been limited by two important features of higher education. First, many colleges and universities have limited success with defining shared purpose. This is especially true at large public universities that have diverse stakeholders, complex organizational arrangements, and multiple purposes. Second, strategic planning has often been adopted as a top-down management approach that is in conflict with the collegial faculty governance model of many colleges and universities. The inability of institutions to articulate their goals and purposes in simple and understandable terms has made it difficult for them to provide compelling evidence of institutional effectiveness. This, in turn, has given rise to governmental attempts to impose external criteria for performance appraisal.

In the early 1980s, state governments' interest began to grow in what had become the largest component of higher education in the United States, state-funded colleges and universities. Between 1961 and 1980, public institutions' share of postsecondary enrollments increased from 62 percent to 78 percent, with an average annual growth rate of 7.1 percent compared to a 2.7 percent annual growth rate for private postsecondary institutions. During the 1980s, public sector postsecondary enrollments grew by a total of 20 percent while corresponding state appropriations increased by 60 percent and tuition and fee revenues increased by 146 percent (National Center for Education Statistics, 1992). Alarmed by the pace of growth in financial resource demands relative to enrollments, several states, such as Tennessee, and later New Jersey and Virginia, led the call for student outcomes assessment programs that would demonstrate the effect of college on students.

The development of assessment practices has taken many different shapes and forms (see Ewell, 1983; Banta, 1988; Banta and others, 1993). Since 1985, most colleges and universities have been required by state mandate or regional accreditation requirements to put assessment programs in place. Increasingly, assessment is being recognized for its inherent value. Whereas the resource allocation and reputational aspects of higher education have remained primarily an administrative issue, outcomes assessment practices have penetrated more deeply into the faculty realm of academic programming and instruction. Assessments of student achievement in their majors and in general education have drawn faculty directly into program evaluation practices. Certain methods, such as peer review, have emerged among faculty as preferred means of evaluating the effectiveness of academic programs.

NCHEMS staff have played an important role in the development of assessment techniques and strategies, much as they did in the resource allocation arena. In Chapter Two of this volume, Peter Ewell and Dennis Jones trace the development of indicators through the history of NCHEMS' work in evaluating higher education systems.

The growth and diversification of student outcomes assessment proceeds in the United States, as does the continued development of resource allocation and management methods and the further elaboration of reputational rankings and peer comparisons. Unfortunately, these efforts are continuing along separate, often uncoordinated paths. In recent years, process-oriented evaluation methods, labeled variously as continuous process improvement (CPI) or total quality management (TQM), have joined the wide array of methods that characterize higher education performance appraisal in the United States.

The process improvement methods of CPI or TQM highlight some of the incompatibilities in orientation between those monitoring the administrative and the academic aspects of higher education. Faculty and administrators often differ in their views of the potential application of what are seen as business-oriented approaches to the educational enterprise. Concepts and language that have grown out of business applications of process-oriented evaluation have contributed to these barriers. For example, customer satisfaction, especially in the short term, is not generally accepted as an appropriate focus for classroom and curricular development.

Despite problems with language and other aspects of these methods, there are indications that process evaluation methods can be successfully applied both to the administrative *and* the academic operations of higher education.

Teeter and Lozier (1993) assembled more than twenty case studies of quality improvement methods applied to higher education programs. In the fourth chapter of this volume, Michael Dooris and Deborah Teeter illustrate the use of quality improvement methods to derive performance indicators for both academic and administrative improvement.

Historical Context: PIs in the International Arena

Performance indicators have a far more specific and identifiable history in the European literature of higher education management than in the U.S. context. The term *performance indicators* was introduced into European public higher education in the late 1970s (Dochy, Segers, and Wijnen, 1990). PIs emerged largely from national governments' efforts to improve financial management via performance assessment.

Cave, Hanney, and Kogan (1991) describe the development of PIs in the United Kingdom and other European countries as being almost exclusively related to questions of political accountability and funding priorities. Legislative and budgetary bodies were requesting evidence of institutional progress in what has been characterized as a shift in the criteria for determining educational excellence away from academicians and toward administrators. Dochy, Segers, and Wijnen (1990) characterize performance indicators as a "public sector surrogate for the information generated elsewhere by the market system" (p. 48).

Multinational interest in PIs has been bolstered by the economic union among European countries. The Organization for Economic Cooperation and Development (OECD), through its Programme on Institutional Management in Higher Education (IMHE), has examined the development of PIs in Europe over the past twenty-five years. Their most recent report (Kells, 1993) includes a summary of PI development in ten European countries as well as Canada and Australia.

The OECD report highlights both the positive and negative aspects of performance indicator development in Europe and other developed countries. In the foreword of the report, Kells puts forth both sides of this argument: "To some [PIs] represent an integral part of modern management; needed by governments to monitor programs on issues of national concern if not policy; and by institutions seeking to make informed choices and progress on reaching stated intentions. To others, they represent a reductionist attempt often by government to make, usually erroneously, choices about funding of institutions or in other ways to compare and to cull rather than improve institutions and programmes" (1993, p. 5).

In Chapter Three of this volume, Ben Jongbloed and Don Westerheijden elaborate further on the European context for performance indicator development. They provide case studies of PI development in Germany, the Netherlands, and the United Kingdom, showing both the variety of these efforts and their common underpinnings.

Defining Performance Indicators

The term *performance indicators* may seem straightforward, but even a brief examination of the literature reveals that many shades of meaning have been attached to this concept. For example, there are different opinions about whether performance indicators need to be quantitative measures with known statistical properties or whether they can include qualitative judgments or descriptions of quality and substance. There are also different opinions about whether PIs need to reference specific activities or processes or whether they may be more general indicators of program performance.

Performance indicators can alternatively be viewed as barometers or "dials" to regulate the supply of resources (Klein and Carter, 1988), as signals (Kells, 1993), or as "tin openers" (Klein and Carter, 1988) to unlock areas for further exploration. They can be used to measure trends in performance as opposed to current value or level of activity (Cave, Hanney, and Kogan, 1991). They have also been promoted as guidelines for making strategic decisions that affect the future direction of an institution (Taylor, Meyerson, Morrell, and Park, 1991).

PIs Contrasted to Other Types of Measures. Several authors have described performance indicators by differentiating them from other types of measures. Dochy, Segers, and Wijnen (1990) contrast PIs to descriptive statistics and management information. Descriptive statistics such as student headcount are measures that have no inherent significance. They lack both worth (knowing whether higher values are better or worse than lower values) and context (knowing how the value compares to those of previous times, other groups, or other statistics). Management information includes quantitative or qualitative data that are related to each other, as in trend reports on revenues and expenditures or course seat demand in relation to curricular changes. Management information adds the dimension of context, showing differences in values either over time, across different subgroups, or in relation to other descriptive statistics. Like descriptive statistics, management information lacks worth.

Performance indicators are "empirical data . . . which describe the functioning of an institution, the way the institution pursues its goals" (Dochy, Segers, and Wijnen, 1990, p. 72). They are related to both time and context and rooted in a goal-driven process. Thus, performance indicators have the added dimension of worth. That is, a measure or statistic becomes a performance indicator when it is explicitly associated with a goal or objective. It should be clear with PIs which direction one would like to see the values go, either up, down, or remaining level so as to indicate the desired level of performance.

Cuenin (1986) proposes a related but slightly different distinction between simple indicators, performance indicators, and general indicators. Simple indicators, such as total headcount enrollment or educational and general expenditures, provide a neutral description of a situation or process. Performance indicators require a point of reference and are relative, not absolute; examples include actual headcount as a percent of the enrollment target and educational and general expenditures per full-time-equivalent (FTE) student. General indicators include opinions, survey findings, or general statistics (reputational rankings or overall six-year graduation rates for colleges and universities, for example) that are not related to specific processes or goals.

According to these authors' characterizations, the same measure may serve as a performance indicator as well as some other type of indicator or statistic. For example, the ratio of graduate student FTEs to total student FTE is a performance indicator if the institution is explicitly attempting to increase or decrease the proportion of graduate instruction. It is management information if presented as a time-series trend or normative comparison. If presented as an isolated measure, this ratio is a descriptive statistic.

PIs and Reference Points. The above distinctions differentiate PIs from other types by their having explicit points of reference. The points of reference are criteria or norms for setting context and judging worth. Some of the authors cited above argue that these reference points are necessarily rooted in the goals of an organization whereas others are less specific, allowing for a broader range of possibilities such as past levels of behavior or norms from other comparative organizations. More specifically, Davies (1993) divides the possible sources of points of reference into four categories: specific competitors, theoretical ideals or norms, stated goals, and past performance. The choice of reference point is complex. It is, in effect, the essence of strategic and operational planning: the choice of what to be now or what to become in the future. Thus, performance indicators are essentially planning tools.

Reference points or standards represent the way in which context and worth are operationalized. They are the essential defining characteristics of performance indicators. They give performance indicators their greatest potential for use and misuse. In effect, whoever determines the performance indicators determines the activities and direction of the system, institution, or program. For example, the Student-Right-to-Know Act and National Collegiate Athletic Association (NCAA) reporting requirements have focused the attention of four-year institutions on six-year graduation rates among cohorts of entering freshmen. If colleges and universities take this indicator seriously, they may consider changing their admissions requirements and programs to improve their level of performance on this particular indicator. This could represent a departure for institutions whose missions are more oriented toward serving part-time, older, or working students that have been characterized as the higher education's "new majority" (Pew Higher Education Research Program, 1990).

Because much of the impetus for developing PIs has come from governments and other external agencies, universities and colleges are understandably concerned about the impact of PI development upon institutional autonomy. In summarizing the future directions for PIs, Kells (1993) predicts that governments will show continued interest in monitoring progress toward achieving national planning goals using performance indicators and other related data. At the same time, "institutions [will] discover that it is beneficial to design and control their own evaluation system rather than having it imposed by government" (p. 8).

Data Reduction. Performance indicators also perform a simplification or data reduction function, reducing complex, voluminous data into simpler, summational measures (Laurillard, 1980; Frackmann, 1987). Rather than poring through reams of data, those who are monitoring institutional and program performance can use performance indicators to highlight the most important elements for review and decision making. This feature also gives rise to one of the major pitfalls of PIs mentioned earlier: the danger of oversimplification or taking a reductionist approach—reducing one's goals to what one can measure.

Levels of Analysis. Higher education performance indicators can be developed for an entire country, a state, a college or university, a department within a college, or even for an individual course or faculty member. The literature reviewed earlier focuses primarily on the range between the college or university level and the national government level. However, as Cave, Hanney, and Kogan state, "The greatest opportunities for performance indicators—and the greatest problems—arise at the level of institutions and departments" (1991, p. 165). This is because the indicators would then be closest to the levels at which the basic operational processes such as teaching, research, and service are shaped and executed. PIs at higher levels may serve accountability purposes, but they can serve improvement purposes only if those who perform the basic operations of the institution use the information to evaluate their current activities in light of potential alternatives and improvements.

Performance Indicators and Processes. Several authors have stressed the importance of linking PIs to specific processes or activities (Dochy, Segers, and Wijnen, 1990, Kaufman, 1988). Kaufman argues that this link is essential if the results are to be used to influence process improvements. Others believe PIs may simply provide more general feedback without giving direction to process intervention (Cave, Hanney, and Kogan, 1991). This issue is complicated by the various levels at which PIs can be used. Attempts to link national indicators to institutional processes are usually seen as inappropriate micromanagement. The same may hold when system indicators are linked to campus-level processes or when campus-level indicators are linked to department-level processes.

The Input–Process–Output Model

Many discussions of performance indicators in the European literature refer to some version of an input–process–output model to explain the role and scope of performance indicators. Cave, Hanney, and Kogan (1991) argue that despite criticisms of oversimplification, the "production model approach is useful not only for shedding light on particular techniques, but also in illustrating the classification of PIs" (p. 32). The authors state that the higher education process is one of transforming inputs into outputs having higher value. Some of the outputs are used directly as consumption benefits and others serve as intermediate inputs into other economic processes. Performance indicators must be able to record information about all points of this process: inputs, process or productivity, intermediate outputs, and final outputs.

This transformation is also central to Astin's (1985) "value-added" concept and to his more general Input–Environment–Outcomes (I–E–O) model (Astin, 1993b). Kaufman (1988) suggests a similar model that examines inputs, processes, products (en route results), outputs (products delivered to society), and outcomes (effects of outputs in community). Kaufman also emphasizes the importance of linking PIs to processes, suggesting that there can be implementation-oriented indicators that examine whether a process or method is performed correctly, in addition to results-oriented indicators, which examine only the outputs or outcomes of the processes.

Carter, Klein, and Day (1992) claim that inputs are the resources required for a service and are typically quantity-oriented (such as money, space, and equipment). Processes are the ways in which a service is delivered, and they require measurements of quality. Outputs are immediate results and are, again, quantitative. Outcomes are longer range and more qualitative impacts. Sizer (1979) expresses a similar relationship between the type of measurement and aspects of the educational transformation process. He proposes the use of economic indicators for assessing inputs, efficiency indicators for processes, and effectiveness indicators for final products and their outcomes.

The input–process–output view permeates the literature thoroughly and is evident in many of the chapters in this volume. In the next section, this model is used to frame the dominant methodological approaches to institutional assessment, particularly in the United States.

Methods for Assessing Institutional Performance

As discussed earlier, there is no single body of U.S. literature on performance indicators per se in the United States. The contributing literature arises from several different historical and methodological sources that can be categorized as resource allocation, continuous process improvement or total quality management (CPI/TQM), and outcomes assessment. Although each of these perspectives acknowledges all three dimensions of the transformation process model, each approaches performance evaluation from a different point in the production cycle.

Resource Allocation. The resource allocation perspective resides at the input end of the spectrum. It focuses on the amounts of money, time, and human resources that are allocated to organizational units and endeavors. Processes are of concern to the extent that they dictate resource requirements. Outputs and outcomes are to be maximized per unit of input. Economy is given highest importance, followed by efficiency and then effectiveness. Performance indicators associated with resource allocation methods most typically involve ratios that depict levels of resources (such as expenditures per student, students per faculty, staff per faculty, or sponsored research awards per faculty). Occasionally, outcomes are included as the numerator (degrees conferred per student who entered six years previously, for example), but in those cases it is usually the quantity of output that is important and not the quality.

The measures for resource allocation models often lend themselves readily to aggregation and disaggregation across all levels of an institution and even a system. Many inputs are closely tracked in operational computer systems because they represent the economic transactions of the institution. This includes the monetary as well as credit hour and work hour economies. Thus, measures are often readily available. Because of their availability, resource allocation measures are occasionally used without regard to context and often without regard to specific objectives for levels of performance. Accordingly, resource allocation indicators serve more often as descriptive statistics or management information and less often as true performance indicators.

Total Quality Management/Continual Process Improvement (TQM/CPI). A process-oriented approach, this methodology dissects each process into component parts and the interconnections among them. Indicators of process quality and efficiency are central to the identification of areas for improvement. Both efficiency and effectiveness are of concern as process goals and objectives are stated up front. These methods make more use of customer satisfaction or its inverse, complaints, to monitor the quality of processes. Many process measures are very process-specific. For example, the time it takes to complete a process, or cycle time, varies considerably depending on the complexity of the process and its interdependence on other processes. This makes it difficult to aggregate measures over organizational units.

Although many operational systems contain process-related data, the specific methods of TQM/CPI often require managers to reassess the types of data that would be most valuable for judging process performance. For example, a student registration office always captures the final scheduling information for a student. Less often does it capture and subsequently analyze the data regarding student requests that are not successfully met. Even less often do registration services personnel ask students routinely about their satisfaction with specific aspects of the process.

In some ways, TQM/CPI methods are performance indicators in the truest sense: they relate to the success or failure in performing a process in the most efficient and effective way to achieve the desired outcome. However, the detail-level view of process statistics makes it difficult to judge the value of the process in the larger organizational scheme. This is further compounded in higher education by the complex relationships among the various academic and administrative units of a college or university.

Outcomes Assessment. Student outcomes assessment emerged from external pressures for evidence of accountability. Consequently, assessment methods focused more on the end results of the educational transformation process: the outputs and outcomes. Inputs play an important role in that they represent the baseline to which value has been added. Processes are also evaluated for their ability to produce the desired outcome. Because college and university operational information systems contain only limited data to measure student outcomes and the processes that produce them, assessment practitioners often use survey research methods to collect outcome information from students and others who should be deriving benefits from the educational processes.

Figure 1.1 illustrates the relationship among these methodological approaches, the related administrative functions, and the input–process–output model. According to this figure, each of these methodologies supports a different component of institutional administration. Resource allocation has traditionally supported the planning and budgeting functions, both internally and for governmental agencies. The TQM/CPI methods have been embraced more within the context of operational management, particularly on the administrative side. Outcomes assessment has been most closely linked with those wishing to account for the results of the educational process.

Theoretically, each method spans the full range of the educational process: input, process, and outcome. In practice, there is a tendency to lose sight of elements of the full spectrum when looking at indicators that pertain only to a single area. Astin (1993a) cites an example of this regarding the use of retention rates as an indicator of educational effectiveness. He argues that it is necessary to take into account differences in entering student characteristics (inputs) when comparing the retention rates (outputs) of colleges and universities. Using a sta-

Figure 1.1. Administrative Functions, Measurement Methods, and Educational Processes

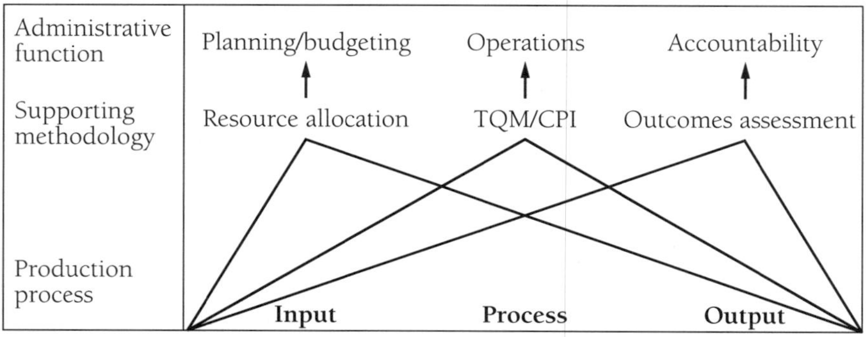

tistical regression model, Astin shows how a college with a relatively low retention rate that admits students who are not well-prepared for college-level studies can be viewed as performing better than a college with a significantly higher retention rate that has more selective admissions standards.

As the European literature suggests, performance indicators require an across-the-board approach to measuring inputs, processes, and outcomes. That is, higher education systems, institutions, and units must address each of these three components of the production cycle and the relationships among them to fully assess performance. At the highest levels of institutional and system management, attention tends to focus more on input and output than on process. This practice avoids micromanagement, but it also tends to lead to management by objective: holding component programs responsible for achieving outcomes without regard to the capabilities of individual processes and the interdependencies among processes. For this reason, Deming (1982/1986) identifies the elimination of management by objective among his famous fourteen points for management.

The input–output view fits with external accountability, where micromanagement is not desired. It focuses on the bottom line and leaves the decision as to how goals are achieved to the institutions and subunits. Because the resulting indicators are not directly tied to process, however, it is difficult to link the indicators to specific program improvement strategies. This also helps to explain the difficulty in linking planning, budgeting, and accountability: unless outcomes are specifically tied to the programs that produced them, there is no direct way to use the outcome information to inform planning and budgeting decisions.

Process-oriented methods can yield indicators more directly linked to activities and their resource requirements. But the focus of operational units and academic departments on their processes is often accomplished in relative isolation from other interdependent units and from the higher levels of organizational management. For example, mail services would use measures such as time lapsed and number of misdirected mailings to evaluate the speed and accuracy of its services. An English department, on the other hand, would use very different indicators, such as judgments of quality and improvement of written assignments to evaluate the effectiveness of a first-year writing course. Although improvements as measured by these indicators might bode well for the respective departments, they do not necessarily help the larger institution reach its overall goals and objectives. For example, mail services may achieve a level of speed that is entirely negated by slow processing speeds of distributing mail within specific departments; the English department may reach a level of quality and improvement according to their criteria that may not satisfy the writing requirements for certain technical majors. Deming recognized these limitations in his ninth point of management: optimize the efforts of teams, groups, and staff areas toward the aims and purposes of the company.

Developing and Using Performance Indicators

Because performance indicators can cover a wide range of levels and functions, several authors have attempted to describe their most beneficial applications. It is clear that the use to which they are put determines their composition and method of calculation. Jowett and Rothwell (1988) observe that even the definition of performance indicators is largely dependent on the perspective taken: that of the government, the public sector, educational administrators, or department managers. The tools or indicators for performance measurement must vary accordingly.

Many of the contributors to the European literature on performance indicators provide criteria for developing performance indicators (see Dochy, Segers, and Wijnen, 1990; and Cave, Hanney, and Kogan, 1991, for examples). Other strategies for PI development are elaborated in this volume. If carefully constructed and coordinated throughout an institution of higher education, performance indicators can be used to focus and strengthen an organization's improvement efforts by helping to communicate a common institutional mission and goals among constituent units and to reduce complexity to manageable proportions without losing sight of the breadth of services offered and their outcomes. PIs convey institutional priorities and set standards for performance and accountability.

The use of PIs is a highly political issue. PIs can be defined as the generation of judgments about performance that are being developed as part of an attempt to reorient the higher education system toward more evaluation in general and more public forms of assessment in particular (Cave, Hanney, and Kogan, 1991). However, the use of PIs has been criticized for overreliance on measures that are readily available rather than those that are most appropriate. This is quite evident in the use by many state governments of credit hour production to evaluate faculty productivity.

Another criticism is that higher education is too complex to make overall PIs practical. This is likened to such general economic indicators as the unemployment rate, where trends away from full-time high salaried manufacturing jobs and toward more part-time and lower paying service-sector jobs are not revealed in the overall indicator. On the other hand, when a range of economic indicators is considered, such as the consumer price index (CPI), index of leading economic indicators, and long-term interest rates, one gets a fairly robust composite picture of the national economy. Furthermore, each of these indicators gives us some idea as to where to attempt to influence change (by stimulating job growth, holding down inflation, or promoting personal savings, for example). Although there may be no general agreement about what works best, there is some agreement as to where to focus the improvement efforts. In a similar way, PIs can be used in higher education at almost any level to promote improvement and to establish accountability.

PIs require the explicit statement of goals and objectives throughout a higher education system. This characteristic provides the best promise and worst nightmare for colleges and universities. If imposed in disorganized or haphazard fashion by those who control the purse strings, they can be detrimental to optimizing institutional performance. If used in an organized way, they can yield significant improvements in institutional effectiveness and efficiency. Assessment must begin at home, within the institution's own agenda and goals, before responding to the call by external bodies (such as government) for accountability.

How can PIs be used effectively to assess institutional performance? How can they facilitate the linkages between planning, budgeting, program evaluation, and institutional improvement? Various perspectives on PIs are explored in Chapters Two through Six, and the editors will address these issues in the final chapter of this volume.

References

Astin, A. W. "College Retention Rates Are Often Misleading." *Chronicle of Higher Education,* Sept. 22, 1993a, p. A48.

Astin, A. W. *What Matters in College: Four Critical Years Revisited.* San Francisco: Jossey-Bass, 1993b.

Banta, T. W. *Implementing Outcomes Assessment: Promise and Perils.* New Directions for Institutional Research, no. 59. San Francisco: Jossey-Bass, 1988.

Banta, T. W., and Associates. *Making a Difference: Outcomes of a Decade of Assessment in Higher Education.* San Francisco: Jossey-Bass, 1993.

Brinkman, P. T. *Conducting Interinstitutional Comparisons.* New Directions for Institutional Research, no. 53. San Francisco: Jossey-Bass, 1987.

Carnegie Foundation for the Advancement of Teaching. *A Classification of Institutions of Higher Education.* Princeton, N.J.: Carnegie Foundation for the Advancement of Teaching, 1987.

Carter, N., Klein, R., and Day, P. *How Organisations Measure Success: The Use of Performance Indicators in Government.* London: Routledge, 1992.

Cave, M., Hanney, S., and Kogan, M. *The Use of Performance Indicators in Higher Education: A Critical Analysis of Developing Practice.* (2nd ed.) London: Jessica Kingsley, 1991.

Cuenin, S. "International Study of the Development of Performance Indicators in Higher Education." Paper presented at the Special Topic Workshop, Institutional Management in Higher Education Program, Organisation for Economic Co-operation and Development. Paris, 1986.

Davies, J. L. "The Development and Use of Performance Indicators Within Higher Education Institutions: A Conceptualisation of the Issues." In H. R. Kells (ed.), *The Development of Performance Indicators for Higher Education* (2nd ed.) Paris: Organisation for Economic Co-operation and Development, 1993.

Deming, W. E. *Out of the Crisis.* Cambridge: Massachusetts Institute of Technology Center for Advanced Engineering Study, 1982/1986.

Dochy, F.J.R.C., Segers, M.S.R., and Wijnen, W.H.F.W. (eds.). *Management Information and Performance Indicators in Higher Education: An International Issue.* The Netherlands: Van Gorcum, 1990.

Ewell, P. T. *Assessing Educational Outcomes.* New Directions for Institutional Research, no. 47. San Francisco: Jossey-Bass, 1983.

Frackmann, E. "Lessons to be Learnt from a Decade of Discussions on Performance Indicators." *International Journal of Institutional Management in Higher Education,* 1987, *11*(2), 149–162.

Gourman, J. *The Gourman Report: A Rating of Undergraduate Programs in American and International Universities.* Los Angeles: National Education Standards, 1993a.

Gourman, J. *The Gourman Report: A Rating of Graduate and Professional Programs in American and International Universities.* (2nd ed.) Los Angeles: National Education Standards, 1993b.

Jordan, T. E. *Measurement and Evaluation in Higher Education: Issues and Illustrations.* London: Falmer Press, 1989.

Jowett, P., and Rothwell, M. *Performance Indicators in the Public Sector.* London: Macmillan, 1988.

Kaufman, R. "Preparing Useful Performance Indicators." *Training & Development Journal,* September 1988, pp. 80–83.

Keller, G. *Academic Strategy: The Management Revolution in American Higher Education.* Baltimore, Md.: Johns Hopkins University Press, 1983.

Kells, H. R. (ed.). *The Development of Performance Indicators for Higher Education.* (2nd ed.) Paris: Organisation for Economic Co-operation and Development, 1993.

Klein, R., and Carter, N. "Performance Measurement: A Review of Concepts and Issues." In D. Beeton (ed.), *Performance Measurement: Getting the Concepts Right.* London: Public Finance Foundation, 1988.

Laurillard, D. M. "Validity of Indicators of Performance." Paper presented at the fifteenth annual conference of the Society for Research into Higher Education. In D. Billing (ed.), *Indicators of Performance.* Brighton, England: Brighton Polytechnic, 1980.

Lawrence, B., Weathersby, G., and Patterson, V. W. (eds.) *The Outputs of Higher Education: Their Identification Measurement and Evaluation.* Boulder, Colo.: Western Interstate Commission for Higher Education, 1970.

Mason, T. R. *Assessing Computer-Based Systems Models.* New Directions for Institutional Research, no. 9. San Francisco: Jossey-Bass, 1976.

National Center for Education Statistics. *Digest of Education Statistics 1992.* Washington, D.C.: U.S. Department of Education, Office of Educational Research and Improvement (NCES92–097), 1992.

Peterson, M. W. *Benefiting from Interinstitutional Research.* New Directions for Institutional Research, no. 12. San Francisco: Jossey-Bass, 1976.

Pew Higher Education Research Program. "Breaking the Mold." *Policy Perspectives,* January 1990, 2 (2).

Roose, K. D., and Anderson, C. J. *A Rating of Graduate Programs.* Washington, D.C.: American Council on Education, 1970.

Rush, S. C. "Benchmarking—How Good Is Good?" In W. F. Massy and J. W. Meyerson (eds.), *Measuring Institutional Performance in Higher Education.* Princeton, N.J.: Peterson's Guides, 1994.

Shirley, R. C. "Limiting the Scope of Strategy: A Decision-Based Approach." *Academy of Management Review,* 1982, 7 (2), 262–268.

Sizer, J. "Assessing Institutional Performance: An Overview." *International Journal of Institutional Management in Higher Education,* 1979, 3 (1), 49–75.

Taylor, B. E., Meyerson, J. W., and Massy, W. F. *Strategic Indicators for Higher Education: Improving Performance.* Princeton, N.J.: Peterson's Guides, 1993.

Taylor, B. E., Meyerson, J. W., Morrell, L. R., and Park, Jr., D. G. *Strategic Analysis: Using Comparative Data to Understand Your Institution.* Washington, D.C.: Association of University Governing Boards and Colleges, 1991.

Teeter, D. J., and Lozier, G. G. *Pursuit of Quality in Higher Education: Case Studies in Total Quality Management.* New Directions for Institutional Research, no. 78. San Francisco: Jossey-Bass, 1993.

Turk, F. J. "The ABCs of Activity Based Costing." *NACUBO Business Officer,* July 1992, pp. 36–43.

Zemsky, R., and Massy W. F. "Cost Containment." *Change,* 1990, 22 (6), 16–22.

Victor M. H. Borden is director of information management and institutional research and assistant professor of psychology at Indiana University–Purdue University Indianapolis.

Karen V. Bottrill is a research assistant in the office of information management and institutional research and a graduate student in the industrial/organization psychology program at Indiana University–Purdue University Indianapolis.

To be useful for policy and decision making, indicators should be developed around sound conceptual frameworks and should encompass multiple aspects of institutional or system performance.

Data, Indicators, and the National Center for Higher Education Management Systems

Peter T. Ewell, Dennis P. Jones

The National Center for Higher Education Management Systems (NCHEMS) was created in 1969, funded largely by federal sources, with a mission to improve the management effectiveness of American colleges and universities. Since that time, the work of the center has reflected (and to some degree anticipated) most of the core concerns and analytical trends experienced by U.S. higher education. The purpose of this chapter is to review how both have evolved, how they have influenced our approach to the topic of performance indicators, and to illustrate this evolving approach with some concrete examples drawn from our recent work.

NCHEMS was founded at a time when states were struggling to fund unprecedented growth in their higher education systems; data to inform planning and resource allocation decisions were a critical need. At the same time, the federal role in U.S. higher education was being redefined through new funding and regulatory initiatives, which for the first time established the federal government as a major player in higher education policy and operations. The decisions faced by state policy makers in response to this legislation created a considerable demand for comparative statistics to provide a framework for planning. From these origins, NCHEMS work went through a number of distinct phases, reflecting changes in both theoretical and practical concerns in American higher education. These phases included developing basic data about higher education, converting these data into information useful to institutional decision makers, enhancing the effectiveness of information use through improved understanding of organizational contexts and cultures, and understanding the role of information in the formulation of sound public policy.

These successive phases have not replaced one another in our work, but have rather been layered on top of one another. Still strongly apparent, for instance, is the basic task of data definition and consensus building. The development of tools for institutional management also continues, especially in such areas as student tracking systems and the creation of quality-management data bases. But a significant portion of NCHEMS current work addresses higher education policy at the state and federal levels. Growing interest in the use of performance indicators as tools for management and accountability has recently influenced this work markedly, as it has affected what our clients and funders demand. However, our efforts in the development of quantitative indicators have always been part of a wider approach to management information and decision making.

Methods and Approaches

From the outset, the NCHEMS approach to management information was intended to be comprehensive, embracing goals, inputs, institutional activities, and outputs. Figure 2.1, taken from a typical publication of the late seventies (Romney, Gray, and Weldon, 1978) remains as applicable today as when it was first developed as a guide for developing the kinds of information needed to inform higher education management decisions. The various components of this general approach developed unevenly, however, reflecting both the capabilities of evolving data-collection and data-management technology and the issues that dominated higher education decision making at particular times. Thus, the seventies saw the development of costing and resource-allocation models adopted by many states, and the design of expansion-oriented tools for institutional planning such as the resource requirements prediction model (RRPM), the induced course-load matrix (ICLM), and student flow models. Greater resource constraints in the late seventies and early eighties led to the additional development of planning–management–evaluation (PME) and program review systems, and to early concerns with educational outcomes and the assessment of institutional effectiveness.

Across all these developments, however, a number of key concepts and analytical distinctions are maintained. These continue to inform our work in the area of public policy, and in the development of useful institutional performance indicators. They include the following concepts.

The Distinction Between Data and Information. This distinction was basic to our original taxonomic and definitional work. The need to standardize reporting first induced considerable thinking about the nature of management information and how to conceptualize and report performance. A simple but fundamental insight was the consistent need to relate pieces of

Figure 2.1. A Conceptual View of the Management Process

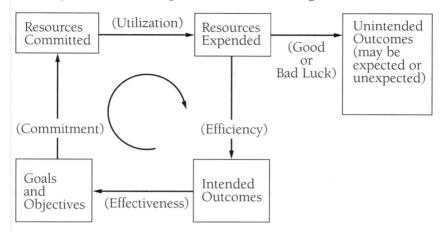

data—often drawn from quite different sources—in order to say anything meaningful about performance (Jones, 1982). This point is particularly relevant to the design of indicators, which typically involve ratios and almost always must be normalized by some other variable to enable meaningful comparison. A similar insight concerned the need to establish and to faithfully maintain appropriate levels of informational aggregation, lest the forest of information be lost in the trees.

Cost/Benefit and Return on Investment. Performance measurement at any level always requires examining inputs and outputs together; it also requires asking who benefits and who pays. For us, this began with the design of institution-wide planning–management–evaluation (PME) systems—often borrowing tools and techniques from business and the military—and moved toward more recent concerns with institutional assessment and linkages between planning and budgeting. Extended to the policy level, NCHEMS activities gradually evolved from classic efficiency-oriented costing approaches (intended for instance, to establish cost-per-credit in a given discipline or function) to the far broader notion of assessing societal need and the resulting societal return on investment for higher education. An early insight in both lines of work was the need to view costs and benefits from the perspectives of multiple constituencies—an insight that has considerable bearing on the construction of useful indicators today.

A Focus on Functions and Results, Not Just Organizational Units. Performance at any level often defies classification by organizational unit or by traditional budget category; it is instead a joint product of many actors operating together, and must be conceived as such from the outset. As a result,

NCHEMS work has consistently avoided building information or indicators systems rooted exclusively in organizational categories. Most instead has centered on the notion of defining a goal (or intended good effect), then determining the degree to which the defined objective has been attained through the deployment of identified assets to support particular activities. Units of analysis for assessing or describing performance are thus bounded by such categories as objectives, functions, and processes as much as they are by particular actors or organizational units. Early work on costing, for instance, concentrated on determining an institution's overall investment in supporting particular cost-cutting activities such as the delivery of lower-division instruction. More recent work has organized indicators in terms of general models of how institutions operate—for example, the inputs–environment–outcomes (IEO) model suggested by Astin (1991).

A major implication is also the use of indicators in combination to present an overall picture of how things are functioning in different parts of the system. Absent this systemic view, single indicators are apt to be misleading. A familiar example is provided by the minority graduation-rate targets for public institutions now set by many states. Without parallel indicators on the numbers of minority students admitted (and their qualifications), fluctuations in these rates may be more a product of changes in admissions policies than of increasing effectiveness in institutional retention efforts.

Choosing the Proper Unit of Analysis. A major conceptual trap embedded in the points above is suboptimization. The same piece of data may have quite different meanings at different levels of analysis, depending upon the configuration and intended function of the system as a whole. In developing performance indicators, we see this most strongly in the need to distinguish appropriate performance domains for individual higher education institutions from those for systems or state agencies. The latter are not simply further aggregations of the former. In developing appropriate indicators for professional training in such fields as the health professions, for example, relevant systemic indicators may include such things as current and projected ratios of persons to professional by region—not just the numbers and quality of graduates.

Similarly, the same levels of performance on similar dimensions may not mean the same thing. Societal interests may not be well-served by a set of institutions that define and maximize performance in identical ways. An excellent, though controversial, example is in the area of faculty workloads—where commonly used credits-generated per full-time equivalent (FTE)–faculty ratios may mask important and appropriate differences among institutions in instructional approaches and assigned mission. At the same time, simply looking at volumes of sponsored research activity by institution may hide the fact that a range of potentially duplicative department-centered research efforts are being supported that might be more effectively concentrated in a smaller number of more focused discipline-specific research centers at designated institutions.

Emphasizing the Linkage Between Information and Decision. Information about performance makes little sense in the abstract. To be useful, it must be embedded directly in a visible management or decision-making process. This axiom seems simplistic, but it has profound implications for the properties of good information. One implication is that the precision of information required for management purposes is dictated by the parameters of (and the risks associated with) the particular decisions to be made. Validity is not just a methodological question. Comparative job-placement statistics in occupational programs collected by means of graduate follow-up surveys, for example, may because of response-rate problems result in confidence intervals that make a researcher uncomfortable. But if obtained differences among programs are large and the resource consequences of continuing investment considerable, obtained data may nevertheless be useful in reaching initial conclusions about program effectiveness.

A second implication is that useful indicators must have face validity—that is, they must be perceived by the user as relevant and appropriate measures of the phenomenon at issue—regardless of their actual technical properties. Sample-based statistics are thus notoriously difficult to use for policy purposes because of widely held perceptions of their unreliability, as are complex statistical manipulations such as those based on regression or statistical clustering algorithms. Finally, to be useful as an indicator, any piece of information should suggest specifically what needs to be done in order to improve performance. Indicators of student time on particular instructional experiences, for instance, may be of far greater decisional utility than generic test scores—provided, of course, that such experiential factors can be reliably linked to actual outcomes.

These themes have been present from the outset in NCHEMS work in data definition and management tool development and they remain strongly present in our current technical assistance and policy work. As the examples of the next section illustrate, they remain living principles, used in combination and applied flexibly to meet particular needs.

Some Applications in Recent Work

Applications of these themes can be found in recent NCHEMS activities at both the state and institutional levels. As the policy use of statistical indicators has become increasingly prominent, NCHEMS has worked both to achieve greater clarity about their nature and content and to assist individual state and federal authorities to develop or refine specific indicators for particular purposes. In our work with individual institutions, in turn, we have not only emphasized the design and construction of performance indicators themselves, but have also devoted considerable attention to properly configuring the kinds of data bases and management information systems needed to support their construction.

Indicators as Policy Tools. NCHEMS's recent concern with performance indicators at the policy level has two basic roots. One reflects an enduring interest in the development of appropriate assessment and accountability measures (Bowen, 1978; Lenning, Lee, Micek, and Service, 1977; Ewell, 1983, 1984), particularly in the realm of academic outcomes. As states in the early nineties moved from sole reliance upon institution-centered assessment measures toward a more comparative basis for judging institutional performance, this interest led to ongoing work on the desired properties of statistical indicators as policy tools. At the same time, our work with state governments emphasized that a determination of societal needs was often a necessary precondition to developing coherent and appropriate requirements for higher education. The resulting needs assessments and evaluations undertaken by NCHEMS staff in several states, though done for different purposes, in practice converged on a number of common data sources and approaches.

Properties of Effective Indicators. As state and federal interest in the use of indicators has grown, it has become increasingly apparent that an indicator must be more than simply a readily calculable statistic. As part of a project on the development of appropriate state-level indicators of undergraduate effectiveness conducted in conjunction with the Education Commission of the States (ECS), therefore, NCHEMS proposed the following criteria for assessing the adequacy of any posed set of policy indicators (Ewell and Jones, 1992):

Policy leverage, addressing the extent to which any proposed indicator provides policy "handles" for action to correct identified deficiencies and signals the fact that a deficiency is present

Vulnerability, addressing the extent to which any proposed indicator is susceptible to manipulation without real changes having occurred in the properties or conditions it is designed to measure or reflect

Interpretability, addressing the extent to which the proposed indicator is face valid, credible, and understandable to the lay audiences that will constitute its likely destination

Balance of perspective, reflecting the degree to which any proposed indicators accurately embody the quite different perspectives and interests of multiple constituents, many of whom are outside the higher education community

Appropriate standards of comparison, addressing the need to establish clear benchmarks of progress or success, based on peer performance, performance over time, or established norms or "best practices"

Technical adequacy, covering the need for all indicators to be statistically valid and reliable, but at least as importantly emphasizing their need to be statistically robust under typical policy conditions of missing or biased data

Practicability, addressing the requirement for useful indicators to be practically attainable at reasonable cost

In the form of both published guidance and sought advice, specific reference to these properties has already proven useful to states as they have been forced to rapidly develop performance indicators systems in response to public pressure. At the same time, these principles remain useful to institutional data analysts and decision makers seeking a ready template against which to assess the utility and adequacy of the kinds of statistics typically generated through such processes as assessment or program review.

Indicators of What? In parallel with conceptual work of this kind, NCHEMS has also engaged in projects with individual states and the federal government centered on the use of particular types of performance indicators. The most important of these have fallen into three main categories:

Societal need or condition. The principal focus for information collection here is on areas in which higher education can make an identifiable contribution to the state's collective welfare. These include such specifics as overall educational attainment levels in designated populations, workforce literacy, or economic activity in designated industries. As part of a recently completed comprehensive evaluation of incentive-funding programs intended to serve "designated state needs" undertaken for the Ohio Board of Regents, for example, progress in a number of such areas was examined over time using such indicators as workforce composition and educational attainment levels by region (National Center for Higher Education Management Systems, 1992).

A similar design for examining state needs was prepared for California and included an array of social indicators assembled specifically to address the differing points of view of educational administrators, faculty, students and potential students, employers, state and local political and civic leaders, and taxpayers (Jones and Ewell, 1992). In the area of two-year college transfer effectiveness, for instance, appropriate measures of performance from the institutional perspective included transfer rates and the performance of former students at senior institutions. In contrast, from the state system or taxpayer perspective, relevant performance statistics included the total proportion of the state's baccalaureate graduates who began their instruction at a two-year college and the costs associated with producing those degrees. Finally, from the student perspective, relevant performance statistics included the probability of students starting at two-year colleges under varying conditions obtaining a baccalaureate degree within a specified period of time.

Good practice. The principal focus here is to track particular activities of higher education systems and institutions that are demonstrably related to effectiveness or the quality of outcomes. Such "good practices" may include both management and instructional activities. For instance, NCHEMS is engaged in ongoing work on the development of indirect approaches to assessing progress in attaining "critical thinking, communications, and problem-solving" abilities on a national basis, as required by the National Education Goals (Ewell and Jones, 1993). Here, the properties of policy leverage and practicability noted above are of primary importance. The case for developing indirect measures of these cognitive abilities rests on both the long timelines and technical complexities involved in developing more direct assessments, but equally on the greater ability of indirect measures to be linked to policy action. Recent work, for example, has suggested that the greatest potential for development of such measures lies in instructional good practices such as the use of active-learning techniques, a highly involving institutional environment, and the attainment of significant levels of student effort—factors that can be related empirically to cognitive development in college (National Center for Higher Education Management Systems, 1994).

Parallel indicators of good practice at the management level can be similarly identified. For instance, among the practices noted as positively influencing innovation in undergraduate instruction in the Pew-funded State Policy and Collegiate Learning (SPCL) project undertaken by ECS were a strong sense of mission and shared purpose, clearly stated learning objectives, and visibly student-centered policies and procedures (Jones and Ewell, 1993).

The proper alignment of policy incentives. The primary emphasis here is placed upon determining the degree to which higher education policies and funding mechanisms work in concert to induce particular—and often unintended—patterns of response on the part of higher education institutions. For example, NCHEMS recently developed a formal policy review process for examining this alignment as it applies to the topic of fostering innovation in undergraduate education (Jones and Ewell, 1993). This methodology has been applied in three pilot states through the SPCL Project. It involves both a systematic top-down review of existing state regulations, reporting requirements, funding mechanisms, and management practices to determine the degree to which these provide institutions with clear incentives for action, and an empirical bottom-up data-gathering effort involving interviews with campus-level change-agents attempting to foster innovation in the context of such incentives. Results of this process suggest strongly that states should reexamine their current one-size-fits-all policy approach to higher education institutions, and that they pay as much attention to ensuring that adopted policies are actually implemented as planned as they devote to designing sound policy in the first place.

Among the greatest challenges in this work to date has been the need to keep the attention of state policy makers focused on systemic issues and conditions. For most of them, accountability has rested historically in the review of individual institutional levels of performance and from this perspective, the emergence of indicators that attempt to rank all institutions on a common metric is inevitable.

Institutional Level. Much of NCHEMS recent work with individual colleges and universities has also been informed by these themes. As in policy work, we have found that the best approach to designing good indicators at the institutional level is to begin with a set of deeply held theoretical principles or core questions and design appropriate indicators around them. However, our work with individual institutions often renders urgent additional issues of data collection and data base design that have a considerable impact on the ability of even a data-rich institution to develop appropriate indicators.

Starting with What's Important. To be effective as a guide for improvement, any institution-level indicator system should be organized around a well-conceived and widely held model of effectiveness. Ideally, such a model should be based on a sound analytical foundation for the area of interest—as suggested, for example, by the scholarly literature on college student development or organizational effectiveness. At minimum, however, such a model must also reflect the values and concepts that are held to be most important by key actors within the institution itself. Not only does such a conceptual grounding allow the creation of better campus understanding of the system's scope and intent, but it also makes it easier for those collecting and using individual indicators to see how they are intended to fit together. Without an overarching model, an indicator system will provide little guidance for improvement beyond maximizing each component individually, however well its individual pieces are designed.

A concrete example is provided by the several indicator systems designed by NCHEMS for individual public universities, grounded in the well-known "Seven Principles for Good Practice in Undergraduate Education" (Chickering and Gamson, 1987). In all, these systems suggest the collection or calculation of fifty to sixty pieces of data, each consistent with one or more of the well-known seven principles. At the same time, such indicators can be usefully grouped in terms of some clearly distinguishable aspects of institutional activity or investment in order to more directly represent the particular interests of distinct clusters of decision makers within the institution. The result is a taxonomy of instructional "good practice" indicators grouped around key questions about decision making at different levels within the institution. These questions include the following:

- How does the institution's academic leadership choose to allocate its available instructional resources in scheduling and delivering classes? For example, consistent with Chickering and Gamson's Principle 1, Increased Student/Faculty Contact, an indicator is proposed that involves calculation of the "probability that a given freshman will enroll in at least one class containing twenty or fewer students in his/her first term of enrollment," as documented through registration records.
- How do faculty at the school or department level collectively choose to structure curricula with respect to content and requirements? For example, within Principle 6, Create High Expectations, an indicator is proposed that calculates the "proportion of seniors graduating without writing two or more major research papers involving library research during their undergraduate career," as documented through senior survey and transcript/syllabus review studies.

- How do individual faculty members actually behave in the classroom and how do they manage the process of instruction? For example, within Principle 4, Provide Prompt Feedback to Students, indicators are proposed on the "percentage of students reporting that they generally receive graded assignments back from instructors within one week" and the "percentage of students reporting that their instructors systematically reviewed tests or assignments in class after papers were returned," based on specially designed end-of-course surveys.
- How do particular types of students choose to invest their own time and resources within the environment for learning that the institution provides? For example, within Principle 5, Increase Student Time on Task, indicators are proposed that examine such areas as the "average number of hours per week reported as having been spent on academic assignments by graduating seniors," as reported by survey; or more indirectly, the "percentage of available library study spaces occupied by students in the time period 5:00–9:00 P.M.

The data from which such indicators are to be derived come from a variety of sources, but must be consciously integrated, inventoried, and assembled. One such system, for instance, uses data drawn from fall-term registration records, transcript analyses intended to document the actual courses taken by graduating seniors to fulfill various requirements (such as general education), a set of questions about student perceptions of the classroom environment and their own behaviors to be included in end-of-term course evaluations, a parallel set of questions to be included in graduating senior surveys, a set of items on teaching practices and course design to be included in a survey of teaching faculty, analyses of course syllabi for undergraduate courses addressing the types and levels of assignments given, and periodic studies of library and other academic support resource use by students.

Although this example focuses on the undergraduate instructional function common to virtually all institutions, a similar logic can be applied to developing indicators about the effectiveness of other important institutional activities. This too requires an appropriate conceptual model. For institutional service activities (both for external clients and for members of the academic community), for instance, a useful model might be based on the notions of market demand and customer satisfaction—how much does the intended audience need and value the provided service and how well does it meet their needs?

The Technical Design of Quality-Management Data Bases. We often find that much of the data required to construct appropriate quality indicators systems is already being collected by institutions, but that results are not maintained or configured in a manner that allows their easy manipulation or retrieval. Needed data elements are often located in different computer files or records systems (if, indeed, electronic records exist at all). Often they must be extracted laboriously from these sources and reassembled for analysis in a more suitable medium. This is usually a time-consuming and difficult task, and one that must be repeated each time such a statistic is wanted. Modifying current transaction-oriented computerized records systems—designed for a quite different purpose—to better respond to these needs often requires extensive redesign and reprogramming.

The primary requirement here, we find, is for a set of flexible, integrated analytical data bases, maintained separately from existing computerized records systems, and especially configured to support the development of performance indicators. Data contained within this data base are periodically extracted from operational records systems at defined census intervals to ensure consistency. Its file structures and computing environment are designed to maximize easy calculation of statistics and performance ratios drawn from quite different sources.

Appropriate intermediate or derived file structures for such data bases will naturally depend upon the types of indicators ultimately to be constructed. In practice, however, we find that the most effective data bases for supporting the development of useful indicators will embrace at least the following:

Term extract files (census data and end-of-term) containing basic enrollment, instructional staffing, and course information suitable for generating a range of flexible historical and cross-sectional statistics

Longitudinal student tracking files assembled on a cohort basis to contain the data elements needed for investigating retention and graduation rates, time to degree-completion, how and when students meet particular curricular requirements, course-taking, and the effectiveness of core or developmental coursework as assessed by later academic performance (Ewell, Parker, and Jones, 1988)

Course/history files assembled on a term basis and containing the data elements required to examine the kinds of students enrolling in various types of courses by discipline and level or the potential effects of offering similar classes at different times or in different formats

An instructional effort/cost file assembled on a term basis and containing information on the departmental resources and costs associated with staffing and delivering particular types of classes under varying conditions

Because such files are designed and built on an integrated basis using a standard software environment, manipulating data to create needed ratios and typical ad hoc queries is straightforward. However, our experience suggests that it is critical to design such a data system as a system from the outset, rather than moving directly into the development of individual indicators in isolation. We have found that, too often, when institutions approach the task of data collection and data base design incrementally, they encounter inconsistent definitions in the base data elements needed to construct new indicators or experience technical difficulties in extracting or manipulating the needed data across different computing environments. Even if the complete design for such an analytical data base is never fully realized, therefore, the systemic thinking that it provokes can prove of significant value in finding better ways to link and interpret the data that are available.

Although the context for higher education has changed markedly in the twenty-five years of NCHEMS's existence, we find that the important conceptual principles of information-based management and decision making espoused in this chapter remain unaltered. Embodied in the development of sound performance indicators for higher education, and flexibly and appropriately applied, these principles are showing new relevance in the turbulent decade of the nineties. Distilled to a single phrase for today's policy makers and institutional leaders to take to heart, their essence can be easily stated: "Above all, think before you count!"

References

Astin, A. W. *Assessment for Excellence: The Philosophy and Practice of Assessment and Evaluation in Higher Education.* New York: Macmillan, 1991.

Bowen, H. R. "Outcomes Planning: Solution or Dream?" In *Planning, Management, and Finance in the '80s: Achieving Excellence, Diversity, and Access in the Context of Stable Resources and Demands for Increasing Productivity.* Proceedings of the 1977 NCHEMS National Assembly, Boulder, Colo.: National Center for Higher Education Management Systems, 1978, pp. 41–51.

Chickering, A. W., and Gamson, Z. F. "Seven Principles for Good Practice in Undergraduate Education." In *AAHE Bulletin,* 1987, *39* (7), 3–7.

Ewell, P. T. *Information on Student Outcomes: How to Get It and How to Use It.* Boulder, Colo.: National Center for Higher Education Management Systems, 1983.

Ewell, P. T. *The Self-Regarding Institution: Information for Excellence.* Boulder, Colo.: National Center for Higher Education Management Systems, 1984.

Ewell, P. T., and Jones, D. P. *Pointing the Way: Indicators as Policy Tools in Higher Education.* Denver, Colo.: Education Commission of the States, 1992.

Ewell, P. T., and Jones, D. P. "Actions Matter: The Case for Indirect Measures in Assessing Higher Education's Progress on the National Education Goals." In *The Journal of General Education,* 1993, *42* (2), 123–148.

Ewell, P. T., Parker, R., and Jones, D. P. *Establishing a Longitudinal Student Tracking System: An Implementation Handbook.* Boulder, Colo.: National Center for Higher Education Management Systems, 1988.

Jones, D. P. *Data and Information for Executive Decisions in Higher Education.* Boulder, Colo.: National Center for Higher Education Management Systems, 1982.

Jones, D. P., and Ewell, P. T. *An Approach to Monitoring the Performance of Higher Education in California.* Report submitted to the California Higher Education Policy Center. Boulder, Colo.: National Center for Higher Education Management Systems, 1992.

Jones, D. P., and Ewell, P. T. *The Effect of State Policy on Undergraduate Education.* Denver, Colo.: Education Commission of the States and Boulder, Colo.: National Center for Higher Education Management Systems, 1993.

Lenning, O. T., Lee, Y. S., Micek, S. S., and Service, A. L. *A Structure for the Outcomes of Postsecondary Education.* Boulder, Colo.: National Center for Higher Education Management Systems, 1977.

National Center for Higher Education Management Systems. *An Evaluation of the Ohio Selective Excellence Program: Displays for Background Data Analysis.* Report submitted to the Legislative Oversight Bureau, the Office of Management and Budget, and the Ohio Board of Regents. Boulder, Colo.: National Center for Higher Education Management Systems, 1992.

National Center for Higher Education Management Systems. *A Preliminary Study of the Feasibility and Utility for National Policy of Instructional "Good Practice" Indicators in Undergraduate Education.* Washington, D.C.: U.S. Government Printing Office, National Center for Education Statistics, 1994.

Romney, L. C., Gray, R. F., and Weldon, H. K. *Departmental Productivity: A Conceptual Framework* (unfinished paper). Boulder, Colo.: National Center for Higher Education Management Systems, 1978.

PETER T. EWELL is senior associate of the National Center for Higher Education Management Systems.

DENNIS P. JONES is president of the National Center for Higher Education Management Systems.

The role of PIs at the national level in European countries appears to be on the decline at the same time that institutions are moving toward more broad-based quality assessment strategies.

Performance Indicators and Quality Assessment in European Higher Education

Ben W. A. Jongbloed, Don F. Westerheijden

This chapter examines the development of performance indicators (PIs) in three European national higher education systems. Throughout Europe, PIs have been employed to different extents in government policies aimed at reshaping the education sector. A consensus seems to be growing in Western Europe regarding their applicability, suggesting that PIs are powerful tools that nevertheless need to be complemented by nonquantitative judgments. This principle is clearly illustrated by Germany, the epitome of the traditional Continental system (Clark, 1983). The Netherlands provides an example of an approach that started from the Continental system but has changed in important ways since the 1980s. We will also consider PI development in the United Kingdom, a higher education system with its own unique steering traditions, where changes in higher education and the role of PIs have been most prominent. For other Western European countries we will only sketch the principal trends. Throughout our discussions, special attention is paid to the two areas where performance indicator development is most relevant: funding and quality assessment.

Performance indicators (PIs) focus on the following quantitative or qualitative aspects of institutional functioning at various levels of the higher education sector (departments, institutions, or national systems): the use of resources (inputs), characteristics of the educational process (throughputs), teaching and research outputs, and effects of outputs (outcomes, impact).

Although performance should be assessed by relating outputs and effects to inputs, many PIs focus solely on the resources, especially the financial

New Directions for Institutional Research, no. 82, Summer 1994 © Jossey-Bass Publishers inputs. Apart from problems posed by the measurement of outputs and output quality, this tendency may also be a result of the emphasis placed on financial matters in higher education policies.

Germany

Germany is a federal republic consisting of sixteen states (Länder), each having a responsibility for its own higher education system within the framework of a nationwide umbrella act. The steering of higher education is a delicate balance between the levels of federal government, states, and the institutions.

Within the institutions, the chairholders (full professors) still have the powerful position they had of old, with a concomitant large amount of academic freedom regarding choice and content of courses and focus of research. Germany has a binary system of higher education consisting of a university sector and a nonuniversity (or *Fachhochschulen*) sector. The courses of study in the latter are somewhat shorter than those in the university sector and are more vocationally oriented.

State funding of German higher education institutions is based primarily on the number of approved academic posts. It is not tied to either enrollment numbers or institutional outputs, but to input factors and organizational subunits of the institutions, with little room for internal reallocation of the funds. An important source of supplementary funds for research originates from federal research councils. Additional revenues are gathered from activities such as contract research and consulting carried out for third parties.

Quality control of the academic staff consists mainly in the traditional bureaucratic ex ante control through regulation: most teaching staff are civil servants who must have the required diplomas and academic degrees (in universities) or appropriate experience (in *Fachhochschulen*) and there is also control through strict content requirements for academic degrees. More important, perhaps, is the traditional peer control, exemplified in the *Habilitation* (a further academic degree after the doctorate that is a requisite for eligibility for a full professor's position) and in the peer-dominated appointment procedure for chairholders.

In 1985, the Science Council, a federal advisory committee for higher education affairs consisting of independent experts and academics, published recommendations for judging individual higher education institutions (*Wissenschaftsrat,* 1985). These recommendations consisted of a list of PIs that, after implementation, was also meant to play a role in resource allocation. However, the list was never adopted for policy use due to the resistance of academic administrators. A small survey carried out by the West German Rectors' Conference verified that in the mid-eighties, little systematic use was made of PIs, not even for internal management purposes (Hüfner, 1988). Sporadic use was made of input and process indicators such as number of students, staff, duration of study, dropout rate, and income from research councils.

Although in Germany PIs have had scant influence on higher education policy, gradually more documents have been published on the subject. Since the late 1980s, the Science Council has regularly published comparative rankings (*Wissenschaftsrat*, 1993) based on the duration of studies (time-to-degree) for selected degrees granted by separate German universities and *Fachhochschulen*. Results point to the relatively long duration of studies at universities, an issue of growing concern in Germany.

The Science Council has continued to pay attention to the state of German higher education, not only through its regular advice, but also by publishing data and indicators (*Wissenschaftsrat*, 1987, 1990, and 1992). However, it rarely presents information as ratios; more often it includes absolute numbers for the higher education sector as a whole. Most of these indicators are constructed from data collected by the Federal Statistical Bureau, which recently started a series on PIs (Statistisches Bundesamt, 1993) showing student–faculty ratios and cost (core funding) per student. Also worth mentioning is the work of Hetmeier (1992), who proposed a list of financial indicators showing some categories of revenues and expenditures as a ratio of the number of students, graduates, and staff members. Although many (input) indicators in his list describe resources made available to the higher education sectors by the respective state governments, others (such as the research council funds per full professor, or income from contract research per full professor) may be interpreted as performance indicators.

For Germany, still very little financial information is available in public documents on the functioning of separate higher education institutions. Very recently, the Science Council took an important and brave step when it published data and indicators on the funding of separate universities and *Fachhochschulen* for the years 1980, 1985, and 1990 (*Wissenschaftsrat*, 1993). This document included as PIs core funding for teaching per graduate and the ratio of core funding for research to research council funding. The basic data are specified according to groups of disciplines and subfields (excluding medicine), but the indicators are for the institution as a whole.

Although they are not yet accepted policy instruments, PIs are gradually becoming important in fueling the debates on the reshaping of an education system plagued by capacity problems that seriously affect the quality of teaching. Important signs are the recent publications by the Science Council that try to make the sector more transparent. However, up to now no information is collected on research output (publications) of German higher education staff. Renewed initiatives by the government to increase competition and selectivity and experiments with lump sum funding show that performance is becoming an issue in German higher education policy. The drive to do something about the quality of teaching is sustained but not yet effective.

The Netherlands

The Netherlands, like Germany, have a binary higher education system: a university sector and Hoger Beroeps Onderwigs (HBO), the vocational training sector. HBO institutions perform very little research, although applied contract research has increased recently. The function of PIs in The Netherlands' education policy is to present information on the sector and to help shape the dialogue between the Ministry of Education and Science (MES) and the conglomerate of higher education institutions about the direction of higher education. The dialogue relates principally to two areas: funding and quality assessment. PIs serve as monitoring and evaluation instruments in these discussions.

Starting in January 1993, The Netherlands instituted a new system for funding the core of teaching in the university sector. Two PIs play an important role in the formula determining the public funds allocated to each institution: the number of full-time and part-time students in their first to fourth years of study, and the number of degrees awarded (master's degree equivalent). Whereas many students take more than the official four years to finish a degree program, including the number of graduates as a separate target for funding stresses the value placed by the funding authorities on timely and successful completion of studies. Vocational training institutions also receive public funds for teaching based on a formula. For this sector, funding is based on the projected indicators of students completing their studies and those dropping out. The funding formulas for both sectors also include cost differences for categories of students (arts, humanities, and social sciences versus medicine, agriculture, and other nonsocial sciences).

Core funding of research carried out by universities is determined in part by the number of postgraduate degrees awarded. As outputs, two kinds of Ph.D. degrees (social sciences versus other sciences) and design-engineer certificates (two-year postgraduate courses) are distinguished. Different levels of funds are awarded per output type. The formulas are subject to correction factors and are used merely as instruments for dividing the available budget among universities and HBO institutions.

The greater part of the fundamental research programs drawn up by universities is funded conditionally—research performance is evaluated through peer review and funds are tied to evaluation outcomes (unsatisfactory programs would lose government support). However, in practice funds are seldom reallocated (Spaapen, van Suyt, Prins, and Blume, 1988). The absolute number of research publications and the number of Ph.D. degrees awarded to both temporary and permanent academic staff members figure prominently in the evaluations. Apart from the core funding, universities can also apply for supplementary public funds for research originating from research organizations, which are judged against competing requests.

From the above description of the Dutch higher education funding system, one can derive the following outline of performance indicators that play a part in higher education policy:

Teaching performance (per academic subject group)
    The number of registered students qualifying for funding
    Duration of study

The number of degrees awarded (M.A., M.S., or equivalent)
Research performance (per academic subject group)
    Number of doctoral theses produced
    Number of certificates awarded to design engineers
    Number of scholarly publications
    Number of patent applications and patents granted
    Number of trainee research assistants (Ph.D. candidates)
    Percentage of Ph.D. candidates who earn a doctorate

Of these PIs, only the first five (as absolute numbers) directly determine a large part of the core funds allocated to the institutions. The funds are allocated to the institutions' executive board, to be distributed using the institutions' own criteria. The research performance indicators in this list are used for determining the productivity of departments, assessing the quality of research, and judging the training of postgraduate students (who, incidentally, are temporary members of a Dutch university's staff).

In the 1980s, The Netherlands instituted a new model of quality assessment for higher education. The Association of Universities in the Netherlands (the Vereniging van Samenwerkende Nederlandse Universiteiten, or VSNU) was made the managing agent for quality assessment and introduced assessment for teaching in 1988. Borrowing some ideas from the conditional funding assessments for research programs, others from governmental policy papers, and especially from the North American experience with specialized accreditation and program review, the VSNU developed an approach for cyclical (every six years) formative evaluations of programs of study. Self-evaluations and site visits by peer teams are the cornerstones of this approach.

Guidelines for self-evaluation were disseminated by the VSNU (Vereniging van Samenwerkende Nederlandse Universiteiten, 1990). Given the formative, improvement-oriented goal (Vroeijenstijn and Acherman, 1990) of these assessments, PIs were very limited in number. The most important PI in this system is the completion rate, or conversely the dropout rate, of study programs. As indicated above, the completion rate is reflected in the funding formula for the institutions and thus is the only contemporary link to government finance in the quality assessment system. The government decided to give priority to the smooth introduction and to the formative goals of the quality assessment system by not tying negative sanctions to negative judgments in either the self-evaluations or the peer group reports. The only vague but ominous threat the government originally posited was that if a study program were judged to be persistently insufficient—requiring at least two rounds of visiting committees—the government might stop funding the program (van Vught and Westerheijden, 1993).

In the last decade, PIs have enjoyed a great deal of attention in The Netherlands. There have been sometimes heated debates about their application in funding and quality assessment. In general, very little use is currently being made of PIs in Dutch higher education policy. However, the ones that are used explicitly—student numbers and degrees awarded—are crucial to institutions in determining the amount of core funds. The small number of PIs is due largely to the philosophy employed in steering higher education. This steering conception, reflected in the normative funding model and allocation made through block grants, is based on the idea that there should not be too much regulation and involvement by the government in internal affairs of higher education institutions (Ministry of Education and Science, 1985). Many more indicators than the few just mentioned are publicly available, but most are used for increasing the information content of official documents of the MES (see Ministry of Education and Science, 1993) and the annual financial and research accounts of the institutions.

United Kingdom

The traditional distribution of authority in British higher education differs significantly from that on the European continent, causing Clark (1983) to call it a separate model. Many aspects of higher education steering used to be controlled by the academic guild and by institutional decision makers, with little influence from government. Changes since 1979 have been drastic. The government has published several policy papers (Department of Education and Science, 1985, 1987, and 1991), introduced new laws for higher education (including discontinuing the binary system), executed a series of budget reductions, and made decisions to increase the value-for-money of higher education. The aim has been to make higher education respond more adequately to the changing needs of the economy and to accommodate a larger number of entrants into the system.

When PIs and quality first became issues in European higher education, most of the activity took place in the United Kingdom. The ascent to power of the Thatcher administration was the single most important factor in triggering this development (Sizer, 1990). Distrust of higher education, especially of the universities, on the part of decision makers was mirrored by suspicion of politicians' motives in the academic community. The British state was evolving from the traditional supervisory role toward a control mode. Distrust within the academic community was heightened dramatically in 1981 when the University Grants Committee (UGC) for the first time reduced its recurrent grants to universities selectively, claiming that it did so on the basis of their quality of teaching, but never disclosing how or on what criteria the decisions had been made. In reaction to this event, PIs gained a prominent place in British higher education policy.

Performance indicators have been used relatively extensively in British higher education policy, but funding authorities recognized that the PIs only partially reflect quality. Therefore, PIs have not been used as the sole input for funding decisions. Human judgment (expert review or peer review) is always an important part of the decision-making process.

Until 1988, universities received block grants from the UGC determined primarily on the basis of student numbers. In principle, the universities were free to spend as they wished. Polytechnics were also funded by formulas, but the practice of earmarking funds for government-specified purposes left them less spending discretion. After 1988, the method of funding changed into a system of core-plus-margin funding (Higher Education Funding Council for England, 1993a). The core is determined by first adjusting the previous year's funding in light of inflation and the efficiency gain the government seeks from higher education institutions. Each institution's efficiency reduction is dependent on its average unit of council funding (AUCF), which acts as a PI per academic subject category and type of student. The institution having the lowest AUCF per enrolled student will receive the lowest reduction in its funding. An institution can lower its AUCF by contracting so-called fees-only students; these are students for whom the institution receives only tuition fees and no government funding whatsoever. The margin represents funds for growth distributed to institutions having well-developed plans for attracting students in certain academic subject categories. The margin also depends on the institutional AUCF. Competition among institutions was also stimulated by a substantial increase in tuition fees with a commensurate reduction in contract funding.

Although the use of PIs for purposes of resource allocation and institutional management has never been greeted with enthusiasm by the academic community, the Committee of Vice-Chancellors and Principals (CVCP, 1985) did take the lead in developing and proposing a list of PIs in response to the government's plea for accountability. From 1987 onward, this list was published annually, containing large amounts of data for separate universities accompanied by a series of caveats that show limitations for each indicator and warn against improper use. The list includes the following indicators (Committee of Vice-Chancellors and Principals and the Universities Funding Council, 1992):

Expenditure indicators: academic staff numbers, salaries for support staff, equipment, central administration, library, computer services, facilities, heating, cleaning, maintenance, careers advisory services, and student organizations

Student input indicators: student load, student–teaching staff ratio, postgraduates (by type: research and taught postgraduates)

Research income: research income per academic staff member

Other indicators: qualifications of entrants, number of degree recipients, time to degree, and first destination of graduates (type of employment)

Many expenditure indicators are expressed as a ratio of total expenditure, student numbers, or academic staff. Student input indicators are by academic subject group. Staff and total expenditure are distinguished according to academic cost centers (department).

The list shows a wide range of indicators relating primarily to inputs. There is relatively little information on academic output, such as the number of research publications. However, the number of publications, among other indicators, plays a role in the research rating exercises conducted by the Universities Funding Council (UFC).

Funds for research provided in part by the research councils became increasingly competitive in the 1980s as quality assessments were employed in allocation decisions. Three rounds of selectivity exercises (1986, 1989, 1992) in which the UFC assessed the research productivity of the cost centers within universities led to research selectivity scores on a five-point scale. The scores were then translated into resource reallocations.

The polytechnic and colleges sector lagged slightly behind in developing PIs during the 1980s. At the instigation of the government, the Polytechnics and Colleges Funding Council (PCFC) established a committee that critically reviewed the current use of PIs (Polytechnics and Colleges Funding Council, 1990). Unlike those used for the universities, the PIs shown for the PCFC-funded sector were targeted at the macro (system) level. These so-called macro performance indicators are not published for separate institutions but for the sector as a whole in order to illustrate the extent to which the sector has made progress toward the stated objectives of the government and the PCFC in striving for a well-managed, accountable, performance-conscious sector (Polytechnics and Colleges Funding Council, 1992). The following outline presents the four sets of indicators that were compiled as a result of the suggestions in the Morris Report.

Scale and effectiveness indicators
    Student population (enrollments by type plus student characteristics)
    Course completion (percent leaving with qualifications)
    Student achievement (percent of students gaining qualifications, plus graduate employment)
    Value added
    Employment and client satisfaction profiles
    Quality profiles
Level of resources indicators
    Index of revenue resource (public recurrent funds per student)
    Index of capital (equipment) resource (grant per student)
    Index of capital (buildings) resource (grant per student)
Efficiency indicators
    Index of output costs (public recurrent funds versus students completing year)
    Ratio of students to staff (students versus teaching staff, plus costs of staff per student)
Source of funds indicators
    Ratio of public funds (from PCFC and the local education authority, including other government grants) to total income
    Ratio of private fees (tuition fees) or research grants and contracts income to total public funds

The PCFC list also gives an enumeration of caveats for the indicators. The macro indicators concerning value added, quality profiles, and employer or client satisfaction are not yet operational. Likewise, some alternatives to the indicator for student achievement may be developed in the future (for instance, by using a course credit system). Such an index may be desirable for the index of output costs because the costs (public recurrent funding) and output then relate to the same year.

Recently, the procedures for the funding of research by the funding councils were established (Higher Education Funding Council for England, 1993c). The funding formula for each field of knowledge contains three elements: QR (quality research), CR (contract research) and DevR (development research). QR, the largest part (about 95 percent), is allocated on the basis of quality and volume of the research, CR is to encourage institutions to undertake contract work on a full cost-recovery basis, and DevR intends to encourage the development of research potential in the former polytechnics. The research grant under QR is based on the outcome (research ratings) of the 1992 Research Assessment Exercise and four volume measures, the latter weighted to reflect their relative importance. The chosen volume measures are research active academic staff funded from institutions' general funds, weighted at 1.0; research assistants, weighted at 0.1; postgraduate research students, weighted at 0.15; and research income from charitable sources, converted into staff equivalent units, weighted at 0.05.

Thus compiled, the institution's volume of research activity in a particular unit of assessment is multiplied by its quality rating (using a five-point scale) to arrive at QR. The research rating by panels of subject peers depends on the quantity and quality of output of articles and books. CR funds are allocated on the basis of a department's success in securing contract research income (not counting the funds from research councils).

The funds for teaching also are distributed on the basis of quality. Here, the funding councils of England and Scotland especially follow slightly different procedures of what in the new British jargon is called quality assessment (note that this is a narrower use of the term than in the rest of this chapter). The common base is that funding council officials coordinate a national process of self-evaluations per cognate area (sets of programs of study or relevant modules in a broad field of knowledge) and peer reviews, in which PIs play a minor role, leading to a summative judgment by the funding council (not by the reviewers) ranging from excellent to unsatisfactory, which will lead automatically to an increment or decrement of funds.

The minor place of PIs in this system is remarkable. The guidelines for self-evaluations of the HEFCE, for example, use the term *statistical indicators* and stress that these are signals prompting questions rather than providing answers. Preferring that institutions find their own ways to describe themselves (within the tight limit of ten pages, plus appendices), the HEFCE requires five statistical indicators to be used in all self-evaluations (Higher Education Funding Council for England, 1993b): entry profile, expenditure per student, progression and completion rates, student attainment, and employment and further study.

The self-evaluations must produce a bid by the institution for a status of either excellent, satisfactory, or (theoretically) unsatisfactory. The HEFCE, after collecting all self-evaluations in a cognate area, then decides which institutions to visit. The rule is that all institutions claiming excellence will be visited, as well as all those where unsatisfactory provision of teaching is suspected, and a sample of the other ones.

The move away from the long lists of PIs started before the end of the binary line was announced by the British government in 1991. The binary line was abolished in the belief that polytechnics would accommodate the intended 50 percent increase in student demand before the year 2000 at lower prices than universities. By granting them the status of universities, the government would put polytechnics in a better position to compete. A year before, the Academic Audit Unit had become operative. This agency of the universities' umbrella organization, the CVCP, was developed to improve the institutional aspect of quality management through quality audits. Quality audits are meta-evaluation: the Academic Audit Unit monitored the universities' quality management provisions through small expert visiting teams. The data these auditors relied on were basically descriptions of the quality management policies and mechanisms, and, through audit trails, proof of the actual operation of these mechanisms. In this approach, PIs play only a secondary role as management information in the institution's quality management procedures.

With the merger of the university and polytechnics and colleges sectors, the new umbrella organization of the institutions has become the Higher Education Quality Council, in which the Academic Audit Unit has found a successor in the Department for Quality Audit (DQA). Practically the same procedure is now applied to all higher education institutions in the United Kingdom. Although for the university sector this is still something new, the former polytechnics were accustomed to oversight of their institutional quality control processes through the Council of National Academic Awards (CNAA) since the 1960s (see Silver, 1990).

PIs may be regarded as accepted instruments in the management of British higher education institutions. As funding is based on funding bodies' assessments of institutions' results, with an ever-increasing part of funds coming from student tuition fees, performance is an important element in the funding arrangements. Since the abolition of the binary system, PIs are reduced in number and play a less direct but still important role in national policies (informing decisions on quality rather than determining them) and are seen more as management information than before.

Other Western European Higher Education Systems

From Organization for Economic Co-operation and Development studies (Kells, 1990), one may conclude that PIs gradually have become standard tools in the management information systems of higher education institutions throughout Europe. PIs are also applied in assessing the quality of teaching and research in France and some Scandinavian countries, for example. However, the use of PIs for this purpose is less frequent. Many countries did consider using PIs such as success rates, course completion rates, and some form of value added for the funding of teaching. To date, however, funding authorities in Germany, France, and the UK have abandoned these plans. For value added, it was concluded that no suitable indicator was available. Course completion and success rates did not adequately reflect the diversity in student entrance qualifications. However, PIs such as number of degrees and course completion rates are currently being used as funding bases in Denmark, The Netherlands, and for part of the funds in Finland.

Quality Assessment

The United Kingdom and The Netherlands were two of the pioneering countries in employing quality assessment in higher education in Europe (van Vught and Westerheijden, 1993), but the third country with such a role, France, has not yet been mentioned here. The French *Comité National d'Évaluation* follows an integrated model of assessment: teaching, research, other services to society, and the management of the institution are monitored in a single evaluation. PIs play some role in that procedure. To improve the quality especially of the financial data, recently an *Observatoire des Coûts des Établissements d'Enseignement Supérieur* (observatory of the costs of higher education institutions) has been established.

More recently, other Western European countries have started to introduce, to plan, or to experiment with quality assessment systems on a national scale. Often, either France or more often The Netherlands has been taken as a model to be emulated, although institutional arrangements are adapted to national traditions and needs. In other cases, more or less autonomous developments have converged to the same models, at least on a very general level. Approaches focusing separately on assessment of teaching or research, as in The Netherlands, are found in Belgium (Flanders), Denmark, Norway, and Portugal. A quality assessment approach involving teaching, research, other activities, and the institution's management, as used in France, is shown in Finland's total evaluation experiments. In Spain, an experimental program has started where all these aspects are addressed, but separately (Garcia, Mora, Rodriguez, and Perez, 1993). Germany, Austria, and Switzerland, as well as Italy and Greece, seem to be lagging behind their neighbors in the matter of quality assessment.

Conclusion

PIs can assist policy makers and administrators in showing the progress made in achieving the objectives set out for a higher education system. PIs are no substitutes for judgments, but are tools used for increasing the transparency of the higher education sector. Because each country has its own particular institutional context and policy concerns, the set of PIs and the state of their implementation differ across countries. In the United Kingdom, a large number of PIs for the university sector concern the extent of adaptation of the sector to the needs of the labor market and to the government's wish to quickly raise the participation rate in higher education from about 20 percent to about 33 percent at a low unit cost. The UK, with The Netherlands, has been one of the first countries in Western Europe to actively employ PIs to legitimize and account for the high level of public funds that go into the sector.

Apart from this informative role, PIs can serve as a steering system. For instance, the level of public funds allocated to an institution may be revised depending on the values obtained by its PIs. As for The Netherlands, the number of PIs actually employed to reach funding decisions is relatively small. This is a consequence of the Dutch steering conception, which awards increasing autonomy to individual higher education institutions, combined with ex post quality assessments (peer reviews). The latter are to a small extent also based on indicators.

If a steering conception were guided by increasing political control and regulation of the institutions' affairs, one might expect a larger number of PIs, as for some period in the 1980s seemed to be the case in the UK, judging from the elaborate CVCP-list. A situation like this immediately leads to the question whether an elaborate and bureaucratic information system can have a detrimental effect on the institution's flexibility and its room to undertake promising new activities. The gathering of PIs can be a costly undertaking, even given the wide availability and frequent use of computers. Informing the public (and funding agencies) of the performance of higher education institutions is one thing, but making them aware of the institutional setting, which to a large extent also determines the outcomes of teaching and learning, research and services, is more complicated. Users of PIs very often ignore these considerations. Those responsible for prescribing long data-driven lists of PIs to be compiled by institutions and their departments should keep this in mind.

In general, the role of PIs at the national policy level no longer seems to be growing in Europe: doubts about the validity of what is measurable, especially if the object is quality, have led to some disenchantment with PIs. More than ever before, it has become apparent that numerical indicators are signals that require careful interpretation before they are used in decision making.

References

Clark, B. R. *The Higher Education System*. Berkeley, Calif.: University of California Press, 1983.

Committee of Vice-Chancellors and Principals. *Report of the Steering Committee for Efficiency Studies in Universities* (the Jarratt Report). London: CVCP, 1985.

Committee of Vice-Chancellors and Principals and the Universities Funding Council. *University Management Statistics and Performance Indicators in the UK, 1992 Edition*. London: CVCP, 1992.

Department of Education and Science. *The Development of Higher Education Into the 1990s* (green paper). London: Department of Education and Science, 1985.

Department of Education and Science. *Higher Education: Meeting the Challenge* (white paper). London: Department of Education and Science, 1987.
Department of Education and Science. *Higher Education: A New Framework.* London: Department of Education and Science, 1991.
Garcia, P., Mora, J.-G., Rodriguez, S., and Perez, J.-J. *The Institutional Evaluation of the Spanish Universities.* Madrid: Consejo de Universidades, 1993.
Hetmeier, H.-W. "Finanzstatistische Kennzahlen für den Hochschulbereich." *Wirtschaft und Statistik,* 1992, *8,* 545–556.
Higher Education Funding Council for England. *Annual Report 1992–93; Promoting Quality and Opportunity.* Bristol: HEFCE, 1993a.
Higher Education Funding Council for England. *Assessment of the Quality of Higher Education* (HEFCE Circular 3). Bristol: HEFCE, 1993b.
Higher Education Funding Council for England. *Research Funding Method* (HEFCE Circular 7). Bristol: HEFCE, 1993c.
Hüfner, K. *Kennzahlen-Systeme zur Hochschulplanung: Die Bundesrepublik Deutschland im internationalen Vergleich.* Berlin: Westdeutsche Rektorenkonferenz, 1988.
Kells, H. R. (ed.). *The Development of Performance Indicators for Higher Education.* Paris: Organization for Economic Co-operation and Development, 1990.
Ministry of Education and Science. *Hoger Onderwijs: Autonomie en Kwaliteit* (Higher Education: Autonomy and Quality). Zoetermeer: Ministry of Education and Science, 1985.
Ministry of Education and Science. *Feiten en Cijfers* (Facts and figures). Zoetermeer: Ministry of Education and Science, 1993.
Polytechnics and Colleges Funding Council. *Performance Indicators: Report of a Committee of Enquiry Chaired by Mr. Alfred Morris.* Bristol: PCFC, 1990.
Polytechnics and Colleges Funding Council. *Macro Performance Indicators.* Bristol: PCFC, 1992.
Silver, H. *A Higher Education: The Council for National Academic Awards and British Higher Education 1964–1989.* London: Falmer, 1990.
Sizer, J. "Funding Councils and Performance Indicators in Quality Assessment in the United Kingdom," in L.C.J. Goedegebuure, P.A.M. Maassen, and D.F. Westerheijden (eds.), *Peer Review and Performance Indicators: Quality Assessment in British and Dutch Higher Education.* Utrecht: Lemma, 1990.
Spaapen, J. B., van Suyt, C.A.M., Prins, A.A.M., and Blume, S. S. *Evaluatie van vijf jaar Voorwaardelijke Financiering* (Evaluation of Five Years Conditional Funding). Zoetermeer: Ministry of Education and Science, 1988.
Statistisches Bundesamt. *Hochschulstatistische Kennzahlen 1980–1990.* Wiesbaden: Statistisches Bundesamt, 1993.
van Vught, F. A., and Westerheijden, D. F. *Quality Management and Quality Assurance in European Higher Education: Methods and Mechanisms.* Luxembourg: Office for Official Publications of the European Communities, 1993.
Vereniging van Samenwerkende Nederlandse Universiteiten. *Guide for External Program Review.* Utrecht: VSNU, 1990.
Vroeijenstijn, A. I., and Acherman, J. A. "Control Oriented versus Improvement Oriented Quality Assessment," in L.C.J. Goedegebuure, P.A.M. Maassen, and D. F. Westerheijden (eds.), *Peer Review and Performance Indicators: Quality Assessment in British and Dutch Higher Education.* Utrecht: Lemma, 1990.
Wissenschaftsrat. *Empfehlungen zum Wettbewerb im deutschen Hochschulsystem.* Köln: Wissenschaftsrat, 1985.
Wissenschaftsrat. *Eckdaten zur Lage der Hochschulen.* Köln: Wissenschaftsrat, 1987, 1990, 1992.
Wissenschaftsrat. *Daten und Kennzahlen zur finanziellen Ausstattung der Hochschulen.* Köln: Wissenschaftsrat, 1993.

BEN W. A. JONGBLOED is coordinator of economics and finance of higher education at the Center for Higher Education Policy Studies (CHEPS), University of Twente, The Netherlands.

DON F. WESTERHEIJDEN is coordinator of research and management of quality at the Center for Higher Education Policy Studies (CHEPS), University of Twente, The Netherlands.

Total Quality Management's approaches to the assessment of per-formance can extend and build upon the ways in which indicators have long been used by planners and institutional researchers.

Total Quality Management Perspective on Assessing Institutional Performance

Michael J. Dooris, Deborah J. Teeter

Other contributors to this volume have pointed out that higher education administrators have much experience with the use of performance indicators as guides to policy. Many institutions have a fairly long history of incorporating data systematically into their institutional decision-making processes. This chapter connects these familiar uses of performance indicators with higher education's more recent interest in Total Quality Management (TQM).

A complete discussion of TQM in higher education is impossible here; other sources examine principles and provide practical advice about TQM on campus (Sherr and Teeter, 1991; Teeter and Lozier, 1993). Very briefly, TQM provides a set of principles and tools that organizations can use to pursue quality consciously and systematically. The foundations of TQM are as follows: develop a mission and create a vision, focus on the customer, focus on process improvement, use systematic analysis, promote collaboration, and recognize the organization as a system. Two of these ideas are especially relevant to the use of performance indicators: the emphasis on processes as well as outcomes and the importance of systematic analysis. With TQM, these emphases have provided a new dimension in the use of indicators to assess institutional performance.

Because they are drawn from business management, these principles should be adapted to fit the needs and culture of higher education and the organizational traits of individual institutions. For example, at The Pennsylvania State University, an existing annual strategic planning process has been evolving continuously since 1983. That process has relied upon a wide range of internal and external indicators of institutional performance, and in many ways planning provided a framework for the university's more recent TQM initiatives. The guidelines that Penn State's provost sends to each planning unit (such as a school or college) now ask every unit to report on its critical processes as part of the strategic planning materials that are prepared and reviewed annually. Thus, planning, TQM, and performance indicators are not treated as discrete tools, but as parts of the overall approach to institutional improvement.

Dan Seymour, one of the leading proponents for TQM on campus, recently noted that this movement seems to be stalling (Seymour, 1994). In his judgment, the slowdown is partly due to the fact that much of the literature and many of the workshops to date have been descriptive. We agree with that view. Sharing stories is fine, but people in higher education who now understand the philosophy of TQM need more specific advice about how to radically reexamine and improve processes on campus. This chapter is therefore both descriptive and prescriptive, as we offer suggestions about the use of performance indicators in TQM.

Quality on Campus

Beginning in the early 1980s, many colleges and universities initiated strategic planning programs. Through the early 1990s, a number of institutions—Colorado State University, Fox Valley Technical College, the North Dakota University System, Oregon State University, Samford University, the University of Kansas, the University of Michigan, the University of Pennsylvania, and the University of Wisconsin, among others—have committed to TQM efforts. This chapter draws heavily, although not exclusively, on illustrations from Penn State.

As of early 1994, Penn State is about three years into the quality movement. The senior leaders of the university spearheaded an effort to integrate the precepts of TQM (called Continuous Quality Improvement at Penn State) into long-term management and day-to-day operations. The provost identified about a dozen university-level critical processes as targets for improvement. These include both academic processes (such as teaching, learning, research, and scholarship) and academic support (such as creating a diverse work force and facilities planning).

At Penn State and in reports from other universities with TQM initiatives, we find healthy skepticism about the quality movement. A few of the criticisms are especially relevant to the use of performance indicators. One hurdle to the acceptance of TQM is the perceived difficulty of finding indicators that can be useful for higher education's core processes. There is a tacit and reasonable assumption that performance indicators might be appropriate for relatively concrete service processes, such as billing or registration, but that they are less helpful given the complexity and ambiguities of academic processes. This consideration is important and legitimate. Because academic processes are at the core of a college or university, such a limitation would be a serious flaw in the pursuit of TQM on campus. We have found that evaluation criteria can be usefully developed for both academic and support processes; we will return to this point later in the chapter.

In many respects, TQM is nothing new. Rather, it embraces principles of good practice, but enhances them by placing them in an encompassing managerial philosophy. This has implications for the use of performance indicators. For example, a fundamental precept of TQM that is most relevant to this chapter is to act on evidence. The seasoned institutional researcher might well ask, "So what's new?" Some other goals are embedded in institutional research (IR) and planning, such as providing required state and federal data. However, providing information to inform decisions—in other words, providing the evidence on which to act—is the basis for what we do and have been doing all along.

The TQM perspective on assessing institutional performance is not independent of the reasons that information has been used and continues to be used in university decision making. This is true whether one is discussing indicators in relation to academic planning, TQM, budgeting, or facilities planning. Having said that, is there any TQM perspective on assessing institutional performance? What is different about that perspective? In what ways are traditional uses of data similar to, different from, or related to how we use indicators in TQM? What are some specific examples?

Traditional Versus TQM Uses of Indicators

Indicators have long been used widely and in a variety of ways: rankings and comparisons, such as those published by *U.S. News and World Report* and the National Science Foundation; institutional data exchanges; individual student and faculty evaluations; studies of student attrition and retention; accreditation-related self studies; enrollment projections; and analyses of faculty salaries. For lack of a better term, we label measures of this sort *traditional*.

These traditional uses are important and certain to remain on the scene for practitioners of planning and institutional research. Traditional measures are in some respects similar to, and in other respects different from, indicators geared to the principles of quality.

We have already stated that TQM entails, to a large extent, a natural continuation of the traditional use of evaluative measures. But despite considerable overlap, TQM also involves some differences in how and why these mechanisms are developed and used. Figure 4.1 illustrates some of those differences.

As suggested in Figure 4.1, the goal of the traditional use of data is often to rank a department or institution in relation to its peers. That is only a secondary reason for using indicators in TQM, which instead focuses on process

Figure 4.1. Traditional Versus TQM Uses of Indicators

Traditional	TQM
Rankings	Improvement
Inputs/outputs	Processes
Static	Dynamic
Resources	Stakeholders/customers
Examples	Examples
Competitive analysis	Process benchmarking
SWOT evaluation	Assessment of teaching and learning

improvement. TQM has its roots in statistical quality control methodologies and it requires that changes be based on fact rather than on conjecture or intuition. Data are needed to learn about and understand processes, not to dress up "brag sheets." The attempt to achieve continuous improvement should ultimately affect how a department or institution is recognized among its peers.

There are also differences in how indicators are used. Traditional measures often examine inputs and outputs such as admissions, student headcounts, degrees awarded, or student–faculty ratios. TQM tries to deal instead with critical processes: teaching and learning, research, scholarship, faculty recruitment and development, or enrollment management. As a result, the information provided by a traditional static measure such as faculty FTE, though still valuable, must be supplemented by more dynamic indicators in TQM. For example, in addition to familiar snapshot measures, TQM might use change, flow, or process-oriented measures of cycle time, customer satisfaction, error rates, or student development. How many minutes are required to process a student refund? How many days does it take to notify applicants of admissions decisions? What percentage of research accounts are lost due to billing errors? What percentage of students are succeeding on standardized licensing examinations? What is the point-of-service satisfaction with student services?

Finally, Figure 4.1 suggests that the traditional approach is often heavily resource-oriented, looking at spending per student or entering SAT scores, whereas TQM is more focused on the needs of stakeholders such as students, faculty, taxpayers, or alumni.

Examples of the traditional approach include competitive or comparative analyses and the SWOT evaluation of Strengths, Weaknesses, Opportunities, and Threats. By contrast, the TQM approach may entail comparing a critical process of an organization to best-in-class benchmarks.

A benchmark is a reference point, a goal or aspiration, against which performance can be evaluated. The comparison against best-in-class may be valuable for many aspects of a university, school, or department; such uses of competitive and comparative analyses have been staples of IR for many years. In particular, comparative or competitive indicators of inputs and outputs may trigger awareness that a process is a candidate for improvement.

To improve a process requires an understanding of how inputs are converted to outputs. The activity of converting inputs to outputs is often represented by a black box, and in the past has typically been ignored. In TQM, benchmarking a process requires that the "black box" be examined. Ideas for improvements may be suggested through an understanding of how a similar process operates in an organization that produces notable results.

Let's examine how the philosophy of TQM converges with the assessment of teaching and learning. Here, the best-in-class approach could lead to examinations of the means by which teaching and learning occur, such as delivery of large lectures or small discussion sections, lab experiences, video education, or distance learning. The examination of such goals as skill, knowledge, and performance established by departmental faculty for all students in a given major, and comparison with other institutions, may suggest that a process warrants attention for improvement. Although best-in-class benchmarking is one of the most widely recognized practices of TQM, input and output comparisons may be more usefully thought of as keys to determining which processes should be improved first.

The National Center for Higher Education Management Systems has done a preliminary study on the feasibility of developing a set of good practice indicators in undergraduate education (National Center for Higher Education Management Systems, 1993). This early work has found some promise in the idea of developing a set of instructional process indicators drawn from sources such as student and faculty questionnaires, transcript studies, and examinations.

Best-in-class benchmarking for a university's business or service operations, as opposed to academic processes, may be easier to accomplish. Even here, of course, the collection of information from other institutions can be time-consuming and troublesome.

An attempt to identify best practices in business and service operations is being sponsored by the National Association of College and University Business Officers (National Association of College and University Business Officers, 1993). The project aims to provide comparative data that will describe a spectrum of performance in more than thirty-five functional areas. Using such information, a college or university could see which of their operations are superior and where there are opportunities for improvement.

Already available is a large universe of data that are not, strictly speaking, TQM process measures, but can nonetheless be potentially useful from a TQM perspective as trigger indicators. For example, an assessment of institutional performance might include an evaluation of financial vitality. Figure 4.2 summarizes ten fairly traditional criteria (that is, not necessarily strict process measures)

Figure 4.2. Financial Hardship Criteria

A 5 percent decline in FTE enrollment for three or more years

Endowment less than expenses for two years or longer

Decline in gifts and donations for two years

Decrease in surrounding area employment or business activity for two or more years

Deferral of 50 percent of annual plant and equipment repair and maintenance for two years or longer

A 10 percent rise in energy costs for the past three years

Tuition income/total expense exceeding 60 percent for at least two years

Net worth/debt declining for two or more years

Expendable funds/plant debt being lower than 1:1 for two or more years

A decline in gifts and grants/total expense ratio for three years or longer

Source: Hamlin and Hungerford, 1988.

that Hamlin and Hungerford (1988) suggest for evaluating the overall financial health of an institution. One of the tenets of TQM is to steal shamelessly. Indicators designed for other purposes, such as those suggested in Figure 4.2, are not TQM process measures, but they can signal when processes need attention.

Another quality concern might be the process of, and provisions for, facility renewal and adaptation of an institution. A joint effort of the Society for College and University Planning, the Association of Physical Plant Administrators of Colleges and Universities, the National Association of College and University Business Officers, and the firm of Coopers and Lybrand has addressed this issue. Their study (Dunn, 1989) suggested that 1.5 percent to 2.5 percent of plant replacement cost should be allocated annually for renewal and .5 percent to 1.5 percent of plant replacement cost should be allocated annually for plant adaptation. Again, these guidelines are probable not, stictly speaking, process measures. However, indicators such as these can also be useful triggers. They can point to areas of the institution where processes may need attention if the quality of performance is to be sustained or improved.

In short, analysts need not necessarily invent criteria for assessing institutional performance, but can draw upon the work of others. Not only does this practice allow researchers to avoid reinventing the wheel, but it also, perhaps more importantly, allows them to focus their comparisons on how people at other colleges and universities go about improving processes. The distinction between competitive analysis of data and the benchmarking of practices is an important one, and one that can be easily overlooked in light of the natural desire to "see where we stand," and to "find out how we stack up." Process benchmarking can help to discover why some institutions are especially successful on particular dimensions of institutional performance and to identify what an institution can do to improve its own processes.

Performance indicators can be develped for academic processes as well as for service processes. For example, one might examine undergraduate education through questions such as How much time do students study out of class? What percentage of students know at least one faculty member well enough to ask for a letter of reference? How many hours per week do students spend in the library? What is the level and frequency of student contact with regular full-time faculty? How many students are involved informal undergraduate research? How many faculty members use mechanisms such as one-minute papers from students for frequent, fast feedback? How many pages of course-related writing are required per semester? What proportion of students have at least one small class in a semester? These questions are different from those addressed by traditional peer comparisons because they focus on the processes by which learning occurs, how it can be improved, and, by repeated measures, whether that improvement is occurring.

TQM and Performance Indicators at Penn State

Penn State's existing strategic planning process provided a framework for the university's more recent quality initiatives. Because of the institution's history of planning, the university and its various units already had in place well-understood and accepted statements of values, vision, mission, and goals when it embarked upon TQM in 1991.

The step from having goals to incorporating the ideas of TQM is not a small one. However, some institutional framework-such as planning and budgeting-facilitates the incorporation of TQM principles into an organization and the use of TQM and performance indicators across a college or university.

TQM supports, and gains support from, mature and accepted planning structures and processes. At Penn State, the emphasis on data and information, decisions at the level of implementation, and faculty and staff involvement are consistent with both TQM and strategic planning principles. Likewise, the university's statement of vision—"To be one of the nation's preeminent public universities, offering the highest quality educational experiences"—is a driver both for TQM and planning.

At Penn State, from fall 1991 through fall 1993, eighty-seven teams worked formally through the university's Continuous Quality Improvement (CQI) Center. As has been true of TQM or CQI efforts at other colleges and universities, most (but not all) of these teams dealt with relatively concrete service and support processes rather than with teaching, learning, research, or scholarship. The following vignettes describe a few of the teams and the performance indicators they examined.

General Stores. General Stores is Penn State's internal purchasing, warehousing, and distribution operation. Surveys conducted by a TQM team revealed that General Stores' customers (that is, faculty and staff in offices throughout the university) felt that the catalog was too complicated. Customers also complained that delivery times were too long. In response to these findings, General Stores staff revamped the catalog and reduced inventories by over 50 percent. As a result, measurable improvements were found on three key indicators: delivery time, employee morale in General Stores, and customer satisfaction. Deliveries that formerly took one month are currently completed in as little as forty-eight hours or up to a maximum of two weeks, depending on the nature of the item.

University Health Services. Another team examined various aspects, such as privacy and time to completion, of service to students at the university's health center and pharmacy. In addition to surveying students about their satisfaction with these services, the team looked at more objective measures such as customer waiting time, both initially and after making improvements—in this case, changing the waiting room and queuing configuration.

Undergraduate Physics. A team of faculty, staff, and students undertook a study of the learning of physics by undergraduate engineering majors. Over a two-year period, the team analyzed a variety of indicators, such as self-reported study time, satisfaction with different aspects of the course such as lectures and recitations, class attendance, frequency of out-of-class contact, and performance on tests. Based on those analyses, courses have been revised, with additional changes still under way and still being monitored. Self-reported study time has increased (in one course, from three to five hours per week to five to eight hours per week) and student satisfaction with introductory physics is rising slightly. However, other indicators have not yet shown substantial improvement. For example, the learning of basic physics can be estimated objectively fairly well using a standard conceptual test widely accepted in this discipline. Although some improvement has been documented with this instrument, the team is not yet satisfied. Also, out-of-class contact between students and instructors remains discouragingly low. The team continues to monitor the effects of innovations.

Alumni Association. When students graduate from Penn State, they are awarded a free one-year membership in the Alumni Association. Before the work of an alumni office CQI team, the office staff needed approximately nine months to validate the accuracy of their records on recent graduates. The team discovered that many errors occurred because student records were transferred from the registrar's office to the alumni office six weeks before graduation, although changes in the list actually continued up to graduation day. The validation problem was solved by several process improvements recommended by the team, the most significant being that student records are now transferred after graduation. The team was able to see improvements in both processing time and error rates, two significant indicators of performance for this office.

MBA Admissions. A team in the College of Business Administration began with the charge of finding better ways to make MBA admissions decisions. Those decisions have been based primarily on quantitative measures, such as undergraduate grade-point averages or scores on the Graduate Management Admissions Test (GMAT), and partly on more abstract qualities, such as maturity and leadership, that customers (faculty and corporate recruiters) look for in a Penn State MBA degree recipient. The team decided that an interview with each applicant was the best way to measure the more abstract personal traits.

The team's next step was to contact six other nationally prominent MBA programs regarding their use of interviews. The team discovered that all six did use interviews, and that indicators such as GMAT scores and interview ratings were factored into the admissions process. In addition, the team discovered that none of these programs conducted applicant interviews primarily for the purpose of selecting the best qualified applicants. Rather, the other MBA programs conducted interviews to sell themselves to the accepted applicants. This subtle but important twist could easily have been missed had the team focused on input or output indicators as opposed to the admissions process.

Perspectives at the Institutional Level

This chapter began by advocating that TQM in general and the use of performance indicators in particular be consistent with and supportive of a broader institutional framework. Conceptually and intuitively, this seems logical. However, because TQM is built around the improvement of specific processes, the links between TQM, indicators, and institutional performance are difficult to show. We know of, and identified earlier in this chapter, many colleges and universities that are undertaking TQM or CQI efforts. We know of none, however, that have persuasively documented with performance indicators a broad impact on the quality of the institution. Some of the attraction of TQM may be precisely in its attempt to be "total"—that is, to improve all operations of the university. However, this vision contrasts with the very real practical difficulties of describing even cross-functional processes with meaningful indicators (Harris, 1993). Finding indicators that capture the quality of institutional performance as a whole is an even greater challenge.

IBM–TQM Partnership with Colleges and Universities. A recent IBM-sponsored TQM initiative sheds some light on the connections between indicators, TQM, and institutional performance. In May 1992, after receiving more than 200 proposals, IBM made awards of $1 million in cash or $3 million in equipment, along with other commitments such as loaned executives and student internships, to nine TQM partner institutions. (IBM made eight awards to nine institutions; one of the awards was shared by two universities, Clark Atlanta and Southern College of Technology.) The purpose of the awards was to accelerate the teaching, research, and use of quality management practices in higher education. The initial report on those partnerships (Seymour, 1993) examined these nine institutions: Clark Atlanta University, Southern College of Technology, Georgia Institute of Technology, Oregon State University,

Pennsylvania State University, Rochester Institute of Technology, University of Houston-Clear Lake, University of Maryland-College Park, and University of Wisconsin-Madison.

The IBM report includes some examples of performance indicators that can be targets for improvement: cycle time in a financial aid office, responses to customer complaints, retention of transfer students, and time needed to deposit gifts. However, it is clear that for all of these universities, no blueprint or ideal set of criteria exists for evaluating institutional performance. Rather, the award-winning universities have long-term, multiyear plans for pursuing TQM (both in administrative and academic areas) that include developing assessment criteria. Those plans entail very deliberate attention to "measures for evaluation" (Penn State), demonstrating "value added" (University of Maryland), and "monitoring and measuring" (Southern College of Technology)—in other words, to very carefully incorporating institutional performance indicators into their TQM programs.

Implications

Perhaps it goes without saying that there is no set of easily implemented, all-purpose indicators for assessing institutional performance. Evaluation criteria will vary greatly depending upon the areas being assessed, the audience, the size and mission of the institution, whether an assessment is intended for internal or external use, and so on. Nonetheless, the examples in this chapter illustrate and support seven principles that planners and institutional researchers should keep in mind as they think about TQM and the assessment of institutional performance.

First, the evidence argues against the charge that performance indicators in TQM merely tell us things we already know or that they duplicate how indicators are already being used. The Penn State vignettes, for example, show a fairly typical outcome of TQM teams. The members of the MBA and alumni office teams were intimately familiar with the processes they were studying. Nonetheless, they came up with surprising results when they systematically looked at performance indicators under the TQM rubric. By tackling processes from a TQM perspective, teams can use evidence to discover fairly significant and long-standing problems and to help point the way toward solutions. TQM is not going to answer everyone's prayers. Because most processes contain the data needed to improve them, however, institutional performance can be assessed and it can be improved.

Second, there is no blueprint or recommended set of ideal criteria, and we have not attempted to provide one here. However, planners and institutional researchers can help to develop indicators that identify the processes of greatest concern at their respective institutions. As suggested by the examples in this chapter for teaching and learning, for financial management, and for physical plant renewal, the higher education literature provides a source of performance indicators for evaluating numerous areas of concern. These existing indicators can be especially useful as triggers that identify processes as candidates for quality improvement. Also, the identification and development of evaluation criteria is probably important enough to warrant serious and systematic attention as a college or university creates an institutional plan for implementing TQM.

Third, in TQM, quantitative performance indicators cannot be expected to tell the whole story. The Penn State MBA team discovered that what matters are not only GMAT scores or interview ratings. Instead, the team was able to learn something valuable about how and why interviews were used by other leading MBA programs. A good job of comparing inputs, outputs, or results against standards can be revealing, but it should not overshadow the need to articulate goals clearly, benchmark processes, and evaluate how practices can be improved.

Fourth, institutional performance indicators often should incorporate multiple measures that use objective and subjective information. The assessment of straightforward processes such as trash collection, transcript production, or billing can be done by plotting a simple measure such as cycle time using the tools of TQM. But a single measure cannot adequately capture the complex and amorphous academic processes that are at the core of higher education. Penn State's physics team surveyed students and faculty, used objective measures of learning, had a participant-observer sit in on introductory physics, conducted exit interviews with students who left engineering, plotted test scores, analyzed the effects of students' high school preparation, and more. Teaching, learning, scholarship, and research are complicated endeavors.

Fifth, as others have found (Keller, 1992; Sherr and Teeter, 1991), TQM can be adapted more quickly to service and support applications than to academic functions. Of the eighty-seven formal teams functioning at Penn State to date, only one, the physics team, has dealt directly with a broad curricular process—namely, how well a group of courses is meeting a set of educational goals. It is not quite true that other uses of TQM have been in strictly nonacademic applications. In various departments, some instructors have incorporated quality concepts into how they teach specific courses. In some courses, especially in business and engineering, faculty teach the principles and methods of TQM. About two dozen of Penn State's eighty-seven TQM teams have dealt with academic support processes such as academic advising, freshman orientation, computerized testing, and the management of research grants. Nonetheless, it is clearly easier to find useful performance indicators for specific, self-contained operations than for complex, amorphous processes. The quality of a cross-functional, abstract process such as learning, broadly defined, is more difficult to portray with performance indicators. Questions about overall institutional effectiveness are especially difficult.

Sixth, the relationship between TQM and the evaluation of institutional performance can best be considered in some broader context. That context may be strategic planning, accreditation, or accountability to state government—whatever is appropriate to the college or university.

Finally, although the TQM perspective on the use of performance indicators is not entirely new, it does bring a change in focus. Traditional uses of data have tended to emphasize comparisons, to deal with inputs and outputs, and to use snapshot-type data. TQM deals with processes and uses more dynamic indicators of change and flow than do traditional snapshot data analyses. It opens up the mysteries of the "black box" that exists between inputs and outputs and addresses the process by which inputs are converted to outputs.

In short, the effort to assess and improve institutional processes through TQM extends and builds upon the ways that performance indicators have long been used by planners and institutional researchers.

References

Dunn, J. A., Jr. *Financial Planning Guidelines for Facility Renewal and Adaptation.* Ann Arbor, Mich.: The Society for College and University Planning, 1989.

Hamlin, A., and Hungerford, C. "How Private Colleges Survive a Financial Crisis: Tools for Effective Planning and Management." *Planning for Higher Education,* 1988, 17 (2), 29–38.

Harris, J. W. "Samford University's Quality Story." In D. J. Teeter and G. G. Lozier (eds.), *Pursuit of Quality in Higher Education: Case Studies in Total Quality Management.* New Directions for Institutional Research, no. 78. San Francisco: Jossey-Bass, 1993.

Keller, G. "Increasing Quality on Campus." *Change,* 1992, 24 (3), 48–51.

National Association of College and University Business Officers. *NACUBO Benchmarking Project 1993.* Washington, D.C.: National Association of College and University Business Officers, 1993.

National Center for Higher Education Management Systems. *A Preliminary Study of the Feasibility and Utility for National Policy of Instructional "Good Practice" Indicators in Undergraduate Education.* Boulder, Colo.: National Center for Higher Education Management Systems, September 1993.

Seymour, D. *The IBM–TQM Partnership with Colleges and Universities.* Washington, D.C.: American Association for Higher Education, 1993.

Seymour, D. Personal communication, January 1994.

Sherr, L. A., and Teeter, D. J. (eds.). "Total Quality Management in Higher Education." *New Directions for Institutional Research,* no. 71. San Francisco: Jossey-Bass, 1991.

Teeter, D., and Lozier, G. G. (eds.). *Pursuit of Quality in Higher Education: Case Studies in Total Quality Management.* New Directions for Institutional Research, no. 78. San Francisco: Jossey-Bass, 1993.

MICHAEL J. DOORIS *is research and planning associate in planning and analysis and a lecturer in the College of Business Administration at The Pennsylvania State University.*

DEBORAH J. TEETER *is director of institutional research and planning at the University of Kansas.*

Key performance indicators are the steering force behind the strategic decision engine methodology described in this chapter, which has been successfully employed at a number of colleges and universities.

Using Key Performance Indicators to Drive Strategic Decision Making

Michael G. Dolence, Donald M. Norris

> Strategic planning isn't strategic thinking. One is analysis, the other is synthesis.
> Henry Mintzberg, *Harvard Business Review,* Jan.–Feb. 1994

What Makes a Decision Strategic?

Strategic decisions are those that align an organization with its changing environment. To be effective, a strategic decision must influence action at all appropriate levels within the organization. To influence action at all levels, the decision must be understood throughout the organization, which requires access to information that defines the issue or problem, familiarity with the context and impact of the problem for the organization, and the willingness to recognize and act on an issue or problem once it is identified.

Strategic decisions occur at almost all levels within an organization. One challenge is to make sure individuals recognize when they are making a strategic decision so that they can align their decision with agreed-upon organizational strategy. A second challenge is to ensure that the strategy is the one that has the highest probability of positioning the organization for success. A third challenge is to furnish decision makers with information that reveals whether the strategy is working, and if it is not, provides insight into the nature of the problem and its potential solution. Decision makers in college and universities and in other organizations serving postsecondary education can use key performance indicators to help meet these challenges.

Using Key Performance Indicators to Drive Strategic Decisions

Key performance indicators (KPIs) are measures that are monitored in order to determine the health, effectiveness, and efficiency of an organization. They are not broad general categorical metrics, such as quality, resources, satisfaction, efficiency, or effectiveness. They are specific quantitative measures that tell stakeholders, managers, and other staff whether the college or university is accomplishing its goals using an acceptable level of resources. KPIs are precise numbers that have one and only one definition throughout the organization.

When strategic decisions are linked with KPIs, they can be especially effective in aligning a college or university within its environment, prioritizing resource allocations and program initiatives, focusing attention, and setting a course of action for the organization as a whole. KPIs allow concrete specification of the milestones and indicators that mark institutional progress. In short, they guide the organization, ensuring that it becomes more effective and more competitive.

This chapter will describe a methodology for linking strategic decision making with key performance indicators. The strategic decision engine (SDE) is a nine-step cyclic method that helps complex organizations make strategic decisions at all levels. It is based on the development and use of key performance indicators. The SDE is a simple methodology to follow. At the same time, it is effective at keeping diverse groups of decision makers focused on the most important elements of the organization's success. After describing the SDE methodology, we will present examples of its application at two higher education institutions.

The Strategic Decision Engine

The SDE model is graphically illustrated in Figure 5.1. The nine steps of the model are as follows:

1. Gather, rank, and cull KPIs.
2. Perform an external assessment.
3. Perform an internal assessment.
4. Conduct a cross-impact analysis to determine the impact of environmental strengths, weaknesses, opportunities, and threats (SWOT) on the organization's ability to achieve its KPIs.
5. Generate ideas that make strengths stronger and weaknesses weaker, take advantages of opportunities, and neutralize threats.
6. Conduct a cross-impact analysis to determine the impact of the proposed ideas on the organization's ability to achieve its KPIs.
7. Formulate strategy, mission, goals, and objectives.
8. Conduct a cross-impact analysis to determine the impact of the proposed strategies, goals, and objectives on the organization's ability to achieve its KPIs.
9. Finalize and implement strategies, goals, and objectives.

Figure 5.1. Strategic Decision Engine

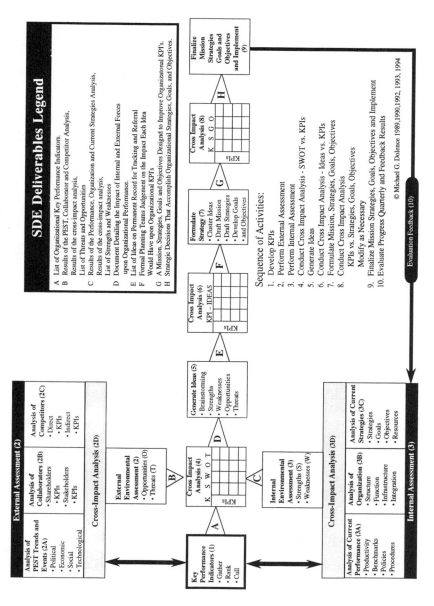

SDE Deliverables Legend

A List of Organizational Key Performance Indicators.

B Results of the PEST, Collaborator and Competitor Analysis,
   Results of the cross-impact analysis,
   List of Threats and Opportunities

C Results of the Performance, Organization and Current Strategies Analysis,
   Results of the cross-impact analysis,
   List of Strengths and Weaknesses

D Document Detailing the Impact of Internal and External Forces
   upon Organizational Performance.

E List of Ideas on Permanent Record for Tracking and Referral

F Formal Planning Teams Judgement on the Impact Each Idea
   Would Have upon Organizational KPI's

G A Mission, Strategies, Goals and Objectives Designed to Improve Organizatonal KPI's.

H Strategic Decisions That Accomplish Organizational Strategies, Goals, and Objectives.

Sequence of Activities:

1. Develop KPIs
2. Perform External Assessment
3. Perform Internal Assessment
4. Conduct Cross Impact Analysis - SWOT vs. KPIs
5. Generate Ideas
6. Conduct Cross Impact Analysis - Ideas vs. KPIs
7. Formulate Mission, Strategies, Goals, Objectives
8. Conduct Cross Impact Analysis
   KPIs vs. Strategies, Goals, Objectives
   Modify as Necessary
9. Finalize Mission Strategies, Goals, Objectives and Implement
10. Evaluate Progress Quarterly and Feedback Results

© Michael G. Dolence 1989,1990,1992, 1993, 1994

Development of Key Performance Indicators (Step 1). The foundation of the strategic decision engine is a series of key performance indicators. The first step in the SDE is to gather, rank, and cull organizational KPIs. Gathering is done in a brainstorming session by a strategic planning steering group. The primary question for this brainstorming session is, What are the measures that our stakeholders and managers should look at to determine whether we are being successful? For example, a bank's KPIs might include number of depositors, average account balance, number of loans, average loan amount, loan default rates, net profits, and net assets. A manufacturer's list might include number of sales, number of prospects, mean time to product failure, and number of widgets produced per employee. A college's list might include number of students enrolled, tuition rate, and graduation rate.

KPIs can be aggregated and disaggregated throughout the organization. A primary KPI for a university may be total number of enrolled students, which is the sum of students enrolled in component programs. Therefore, the business school would have an enrollment KPI that contributes to the institution's overall KPI and the departments of accounting, finance, marketing, and the MBA program have enrollment KPIs that contribute to the school's KPI. KPIs thus form a pyramid, with the organization-wide KPIs sitting at the top, division KPIs sitting one layer underneath, and major unit and department level KPIs forming the foundation.

The group charged with formulating KPIs may at first adamantly refuse to get specific in developing them. They may instead formulate broad general categories such as quality, resources, satisfaction, efficiency, or effectiveness. These categories can be used to help the group construct more specific KPIs within each general category. For example, quality may be measured by mean time to response, number of complaints, or scores on a monthly service evaluation survey. Initially, KPIs should use available data but it is likely that the group will identify measures requiring data that are not readily available.

External Assessment (Step 2). Once the initial set of KPIs is articulated, the planning group is ready to turn its attention to the external environment. The SDE characterizes the external environment in three domains: political, economic, sociological, and technological events and trends; collaborators; and competitors.

PEST Trends Analysis (Step 2A). The first domain is defined by a PEST analysis, which evaluates political, economic, sociological, and technological trends and events. The acronym also reflects how many groups feel about the process. The purpose of the PEST analysis is threefold. First, it illuminates trends and events that may have a positive or negative impact on the organization's health. Second, it furnishes the planning group with an in-depth understanding of these factors and their effects. Third, and most important, the PEST analysis determines the degree to which the organization is properly aligned with the full range of significant factors in its environment. By focusing on changes in the environment, the analysis highlights where these changes can create misalignments unless the college or university takes action in anticipation of the changes.

The PEST analysis helps the planning group avoid three frequent pitfalls of the planning process. First, the analysis recognizes weak environmental signals whose presence is not widely felt or understood by the organization but that may have significant negative impact. Most organizations usually avoid this category of environmental factor. Second, the PEST analysis also recognizes that the importance and impact of each trend and event is different. This allows the group to focus attention on the more important ones and minimize time and effort devoted to less influential external forces. Finally, this form of PEST analysis avoids "paralysis by analysis" by focusing attention on only the trends and events that impact the KPIs. By viewing the environment through the lens of the KPIs, the PEST analysis is much more focused than traditional environmental scanning analyses. The focus comes from the process of centering discussion and analysis on the impact of specific environmental trends and events on specific aspects of organizational performance.

During the PEST analysis, the planning group is likely to discover that it has omitted an important KPI that should be monitored. The KPI is added and the analysis continues. Once the most important PEST trends and events are identified, their potential impact on the organizational KPIs is assessed. This impact assessment is accomplished using a cross-impact analysis, explained in a later section.

Analysis of Collaborators (Step 2B). The second domain of the external analysis is an analytical look at the organization's collaborators, or stakeholders. These stakeholders are individuals and organizations who have a vested interest in the institution's success. Examples include employers, parents, students, suppliers, lenders, employee unions, special interest groups, government agencies, and professional associations. For public institutions, the state legislature and the executive branch of state government are especially important stakeholders.

The analysis first requires identification by name of these stakeholders, followed by an articulation of the KPIs that they use to measure their own success and the KPIs by which they would measure the success of the institution with which they collaborate. A cross-impact analysis of these stakeholder KPIs with the institution's own KPIs allows the planning group to identify win-win scenarios, pinpoint potential collaborations, and recognize possible opportunities and threats to the institution.

Analysis of Competitors (Step 2C). The third domain of the external analysis is an analytical look at the organization's competitors. Competitors are organizations that have a "negative interest" in the institution. They seek attention and resources from the same customers, suppliers, and providers. In the postsecondary education context, competitors include other institutions. For state institutions, competitors also include other entities vying for state funding—K–12 education, law enforcement, prisons, health care, and economic development, to name a few. Again, identification of these competitors is the first step in the analytic process, followed by specification of their KPIs. These activities can take the form of competitive market and peer group analyses. In addition to identifying important competitors, this analysis helps to illuminate their strategies and tactics and to understand how they affect the organization's own success as expressed through the KPIs identified in Step 1. The competitor KPIs are included in the culminating cross-impact analysis stage of Step 2.

Cross-Impact Analysis (Step 2D). The cross-impact analysis (CIA) is a Delphi technique that gives the planning group a clear vision of how a set of factors affects the achievement of the organization's KPIs. The method will be illustrated as implemented at the culmination of the external environment analysis—Step 2D in Figure 5.1. The CIA is a technique for harvesting the collective judgment of the group and focusing group discussion and supporting analysis. It is conducted using a two-dimensional matrix where the organization's KPIs are arrayed down the rows; the factors to be considered for their impact on KPIs are arrayed across the columns. The factors whose effects on the institution's KPIs are to be evaluated could include PEST trends and events, stakeholders' KPIs, and competitors' KPIs. Table 5.1 illustrates a portion of the matrix for Step 2D. Each member of the group assesses the impact that each trend and event would have on each KPI using the scale in Table 5.1.

Table 5.2 shows an example of one group member's assessments of the impact of four environmental trends and events on a state university's KPIs. Examining the scores in each cell provokes questions regarding what reasoning was applied to arrive at the assigned values. Why, for example, did the individual believe that the election of a new governor with a platform of low taxes, low tuition, and a commitment to reduce the state budget by cutting all agencies would result in a strong positive influence on the institution's five-year graduation rate?

Open discussion of the perceived impact of trends and events on organizational KPIs is the first step in preparing the planning group for effective decision making. Compiling group aggregate scores is a useful tool toward this

Table 5.1. Cross-Impact Matrix for PEST Analysis

	Political Trend or Event	Economic Trend or Event	Social Trend or Event	Technological Trend or Event
KPI 1	Cell 1	Cell 6	Cell 11	Cell 16
KPI 2	Cell 2	Cell 7	Cell 12	Cell 17
KPI 3	Cell 3	Cell 8	Cell 13	Cell 18
KPI 4	Cell 4	Cell 9	Cell 14	Cell 19
KPI 5	Cell 5	Cell 10	Cell 15	Cell 20

Scale for rating impact in each cell:

6 = strong positive influence   5 = moderate positive influence

4 = weak positive influence   3 = weak negative influence

2 = moderate negative influence   1 = strong negative influence

0 = neutral, don't know, no impact, not applicable

Table 5.2. Sample Individual Scores for PEST Cross-Impact Analysis

	New governor platform: low tuition, low taxes, cut state agency budgets	High inflation rate and unemployment; new jobs require a college education	Population increase in the region; birth rate increase; immigration increase	Using technology to personalize instruction = 20% increase in grades
FTE enrollment	1	6	6	5
Tuition rate	1	3	0	3
Graduation rate	6	2	0	5
State appropriations	1	3	3	0
Financial aid	0	2	4	0

end. Table 5.3 reports the means and standard deviations for each cell. The mean provides the group response and the standard deviation indicates the degree of consensus. The higher the standard deviation, the more widely spread the group members' individual judgments. High standard deviations reveal that more discussion may be needed to reach consensus. The CIA group scores can also be derived by public group discussion with a facilitator seeking verbal consensus. This approach may not work well in groups composed of members of unequal status. In such cases, a variety of techniques can be used to eliminate status barriers, such as the use of a computer-based decision room or electronic voting pads that mask the identity of the individual and count everyone's vote equally.

The CIA is used to evaluate the impact of all PEST trends and events as well as the collaborator and competitor KPIs.

Internal Assessment (Step 3). The purpose of the internal assessment is to evaluate the influence that organizational form, function, resources, strategies, goals, and objectives have on achieving the KPIs. Organizational units tend to use this type of review to make the case for more resources. This tendency should be avoided during this stage of the planning process. The analysis should be taken as an opportunity to describe the current state of the institution as a baseline for change. It includes assessments of three interrelated components: organizational performance, organizational strategies, and organizational form.

Analysis of Current Performance (Step 3A). The analysis of current performance begins by establishing benchmarks. These can be the average performance metrics of like institutions, performance levels of the closest competitors, or a compilation of the "best practices in the industry." Benchmarks help anchor the internal analysis in performance standards.

Productivity is a second essential element of organizational performance that can be measured in a number of different ways. It can be evaluated based

Table 5.3. Sample Group Scores for PEST Cross-Impact Analysis

	New governor platform: low tuition, low taxes, cut state agency budgets	High inflation rate and unemployment; new jobs require a college education	Population increase in the region; birth rate increase; immigration increase	Using technology to personalize instruction = 20% increase in grades
FTE enrollment	Mean 1.3 STD .34	Mean 5.5 STD .01	Mean 5.9 STD .01	Mean 5.8 STD .01
Tuition rate	Mean 1.2 STD .46	Mean 3.2 STD .01	Mean 4.2 STD .01	Mean 2.3 STD .01
Graduation rate	Mean 0.9 STD 3.11	Mean 2.1 STD 1.01	Mean 2.6 STD 2.01	Mean 5.1 STD 1.51
State appropriations	Mean 1.4 STD .02	Mean 1.8 STD .01	Mean 3.7 STD 2.84	Mean 2.8 STD .26
Financial aid	Mean 2.1 STD .01	Mean 2.1 STD .01	Mean 3.3 STD 4.72	Mean 3.4 STD .32

on performance per work hour or number of FTE staff; it can be expressed in ratios of personnel to workload, or workload to cost. Both benchmarks and productivity measures are interrelated indicators that help institutions monitor the organization's performance. They may include some of the KPIs established in Step 1, but may also include other, less strategic elements. Table 5.4 displays samples of benchmark and productivity measures.

Progress on KPIs can be achieved only if organizational policies and procedures facilitate their realization. Ultimately, every organizational policy and procedure should be passed through a cross-impact analysis. In this way, the planning group can assess the impact of each policy on KPIs, benchmarks, and productivity measures. During the analysis of organizational performance, the planning group should at least review major policies and procedures in this way.

Analysis of Organizational Form (Step 3B). Four components of organizational form are evaluated, including structure, function, infrastructure, and integration. The purpose of this analysis is to gain insights into the impact of organizational form on organizational KPIs. Structure is defined as the authority, governance, and reporting relationships that establish rules of operation within an organization. It is often diagrammed in organizational charts that can be classified into organizational typologies such as hierarchical, flat, or star. When structure is combined with division, unit, and individual functions and analyzed against organizational KPIs, some interesting insights begin to emerge. For example, it could be found that hierarchical, function-based organizational structures retard the achievement of institutional KPI targets for enrollment and retention of students. Analysis of organization infrastructure should include a consideration of the physical plant, telecommunications networks, administrative and academic information systems, and classroom

Table 5.4. Sample Benchmark and Productivity Measures

Instruction	Finance	Enrollment	Technology
Student-faculty ratio measured for full- and part-time faculty	Instructional cost per FTE student	Cost of recruiting a new student	Number of open access personal computers
Graduation rate measure for 4, 5, 6+ year intervals	Preventive maintenance expenditures per gross square foot	Ratio of institutional financial aid to total tuition revenue	Percentage of courses requiring technology access
Percentage of lower-division courses taught by full-time faculty	Faculty salary schedule	Fall-to-fall retention rates for different subcategories of students	Percentage of faculty with personal computers
Percentage of faculty with terminal degree	Annual or per credit hour tuition rate	Average course unit load per student	Percentage of faculty connected to Internet
Percentage of faculty with tenure	Student fees	Percentage of inquiries who apply	Ratio of personal computers to students
Average high school GPA of incoming students	Room charges	Percentage of applicants who are accepted	Number of campus network users
Diversity of faculty	Board charges	Percentage of accepted students who enroll	Software availability
Faculty salary equity	Annual fund giving	Ratio of students transferring in to students transferring out	Inventory of desktop functions

equipment. The final dimension of organizational form is how well the different divisions, units, and even individuals integrate their activity and efforts. The analysis should include judgments on the level of cross-unit integration and communication within the organization.

Analysis of Current Strategies (Step 3C). The planning group should next articulate the organization's present strategies, goals, objectives, tactics, and resources. This activity should be done through the lens of both the KPIs and the benchmark and productivity measures. Strategies are initiatives that align, realign, or maintain alignment between the organization and the environment. They are, or should be, long-term in nature, although they may have significant short-term impact on the organization, its collaborators, and its competitors. Goals are milestones achieved, usually over more than one year, and objectives are more immediate, time-bound, and measurable desired outcomes. Tactics are activities that move the organization closer to achieving its goals and objectives. Resources are the fiscal, human, technological, and organizational inputs to the organization's operations.

Internal Assessment CIA (Step 3D). After performing all three components of the internal assessment, the planning group engages in a cross-impact analysis to analyze the impact of the identified strengths and weaknesses on the KPIs. Again, the CIA is used to focus on the more consequential factors and to achieve consensus on the impact of these factors on institutional progress.

KPI–SWOT CIA (Step 4). As a result of the internal and external analyses, the planning group will have uncovered many of the organization's strengths, weaknesses, opportunities, and threats. In the fourth step of the SDE, these planning factors are evaluated against the organization's KPIs using the cross-impact analysis method described earlier. The purpose of this step is to measure the impact each strength, weakness, opportunity, and threat has on the KPIs. The KSWOT should be a blind vote with each participant receiving a single vote. This method mitigates the potential of having opinion leaders disproportionately influencing the vote. The result of this step is a ranked scoring of the external and internal factors that affect an organization's KPIs.

Idea Generation (Step 5). With a common and focused frame of reference provided by the results of the preceding steps, the planning group is ready to generate ideas. An open brainstorming session is used to solicit ideas on ways to improve the organization's performance as indicated by the KPIs. That is, the planning group members must think of ways to reduce the impacts of threats and weaknesses and to enhance the benefits of opportunities and strengths. Ideas can be contributed blindly and then listed without attribution or simply gathered in an open meeting. One important rule applies: participants must be free to say what they wish without negative comment by anyone. Negative comments can seriously reduce the quality of the ideas. If such comments are observed, the group should move to a blind contribution process.

KPI–Idea CIA (Step 6). Once the ideas are generated, discussed, and clarified, they are evaluated against the KPIs by a cross-impact analysis. This helps to refine the ideas generated in the brainstorming session as well as to cluster them into meaningful groups and determine their impact on the KPIs. Ideas without form or specificity must be discussed and refined so that the group members can assign values from the CIA scale. Ideas of little or negative impact begin to fall out of serious consideration in this analysis.

Strategy Formulation (Step 7). The process of formulating the organization's mission, strategies, goals, and objectives is the culmination of the preceding six steps. It can now occur with a common understanding of the purpose of actions to be outlined and a group expectation as to the impact of these actions on organizational performance. A review of prior step results prepares the group to cluster ideas into strategies, develop tactics, and assign organizational goals, objectives, and responsibilities.

Strategy, Goal, and Objectives CIA (Step 8). Once again, the CIA technique is used to evaluate how the strategies, goals and objectives will affect the organization's KPIs. As with all previous CIA implementations, the group members vote anonymously and their tallies are aggregated into a composite matrix. Cells with large standard deviations are discussed further to see whether consensus can be reached. Even if consensus cannot be reached, the strategies, goals, and objectives should be clarified to reach at least a uniform understanding of their definition.

Finalize Strategies, Goals, and Objectives for Implementation (Step 9). With the final analysis as a guide, the group fine-tunes its decisions and assigns them to managers, units, and individual work plans for implementation. As part of this implementation, responsibility must be given to units to maintain the information required to monitor progress according to the KPIs. Although these responsibilities may be spread throughout the organization, it is recommended that a centralized support unit, such as an institutional research office, be given both a facilitative and coordinating role in assembling KPI results in a systematic fashion.

In practice, the application of the SDE is tailored to each specific setting. The nature of the college or university, its particular set of opportunities and challenges, the history of planning on the campus, and the quality of campus leadership all affect the customization of the SDE. This tailoring affects the composition of the planning group; the balance between different parts of the SDE; and the nature of the KPIs, strategies, and goals that result. The following two examples illustrate the differences in the KPIs that were developed by two different educational institutions.

University of Northern Colorado

The University of Northern Colorado, located in Greeley, approximately fifty miles north of Denver, was founded in 1889 as the State Normal School. UNC is classified as a Doctoral-Granting I university within the Carnegie Classification system. One of twelve institutions in Colorado offering four-year degree programs and one of six providing doctoral education, the university is organized into seven colleges: Education, Arts and Sciences, Performing and Visual Arts, Business, Health and Human Services, the Graduate School, and Continuing Education. UNC operates within an annual budget of $89.8 million (1993–1994), including $30.7 million from state general fund appropriations, $25.1 million from tuition authorizations, $3.1 million from sponsored programs, and $31.1 million from auxiliary service activities such as housing and food services.

UNC enrolls approximately 8,300 undergraduate and 1,450 graduate FTE students. The average entering student has a high school GPA of 3.10 on a four-point scale and either a 907 combined SAT score or a 21.7 composite ACT score. A majority of students live on campus or in Greeley. They are largely from Colorado (about 90 percent), just over 10 percent are minority students, and 58 percent are female. In 1992–1993, UNC awarded 1,613 baccalaureate, 656 master's, and 55 doctoral degrees. The 462 full-time faculty are 39 percent female, 59 percent tenured. Sixty-eight percent of the full-time faculty hold terminal degrees and 8 percent are minorities.

A number of the political and economic factors currently affecting UNC stem from state legislative actions. The Colorado legislature recently passed House Bill 1187, mandating a lead role for UNC in statewide teacher education. Senate Bill 136 shifts more of the cost of education from general fund dollars to tuition and sets a limit on the percentage of out-of-state students allowed in Colorado public colleges and universities. The legislature also recently enacted Amendment I, imposing strict fiscal constraints on all state agencies and institutions. Finally, Senate Bill 136 establishes a new system for setting appropriation levels. Socially, the state of Colorado is becoming more culturally diverse and is experiencing population growth through in-migration and increasing birth rates. On the technological front, UNC must prepare its students to succeed in the emerging information-based economy and global society.

To deal effectively with these and a host of other factors, the university initiated the KPI-based strategic planning system described in this chapter. The process was designed and facilitated by one of the authors in collaboration with campus leadership. The process included more than 300 campus representatives who were brought together through the use of a decision-support facility housed in the UNC College of Business. Electronic brainstorming conducted by the numerous representatives resulted in almost 100 candidate key performance indicators, which were sifted and prioritized into the 20 primary institutional KPIs found in Table 5.5. The cross-impact of factors from the external and internal analyses on the KPIs resulted in a sharp focus in four strategic areas: enrollment management, academic program development, information technology, and university resources and services.

A formal strategic enrollment management (SEM) program was launched by assembling a team to build an implementation plan based on a combination of financial, quality, and enrollment factors. The group's decision-making activities were sharply focused by the effects enrollment changes have on finances, retention, academic quality, and strategic position, which were identified in the analysis processes of the SDE methodology. The insights generated through the application of the SDE and the SEM program enabled the group to set reasonable targets for 1993–1994 enrollment that were met precisely.

Academic program strategies recognized significant increases in competition for quality students. Competitive strategies are being assembled within the academic context of UNC. Competition for resources was identified as another significant factor to be considered. Priorities for action emerged in the areas of making the faculty salary schedule at UNC more competitive with peer institutions and reallocating scarce development dollars toward realigning academic expertise and programs with constituent needs and expectations. Academic strategic planning continues to develop at UNC at the college and department levels.

Table 5.5. Summary of KPIs for University of Northern Colorado

KPI	Current Value	Five-Year Goal	Ten-Year Goal	Metric
1. Undergraduate FTE enrollment	8,271	9,250	10,000	Number units attempted divided by 15
2. Graduate FTE enrollment	1,435	1,600	2,000	Number units attempted divided by 12
3. Off-campus cash funded enrollment	834.8	1,150	1,500	Number units attempted divided by 15
4. Academic quality of entering freshmen	97.7	100	103	CCHE index combining SAT, ACT, and GPA
5. In-state resident students	89%	85%	79%	Percentage of students who are Colorado residents
6. Minority share of UNC graduates	7.9%	15%	20%	Percentage of minority bachelor's degree recipients
7. Six-year graduation rate	41.2%	50%	60%	Percentage of full-time first-year students who graduate within six years
8. Undergraduate fall-to-fall retention rate	77.2%	80%	85%	Percentage of students who enroll the following fall
9. Doctoral degrees awarded	55	75	100	Number of doctoral degrees awarded annually
10. Alumni attitude audit	85%	85%	85%	Percentage of alumni rating UNC Good or Very Good
11. Faculty quality	To be determined by faculty evaluation task force			
12. Faculty teaching contribution	63%	TBD	TBD	Percentage of lower-division courses taught by full-time faculty
13. Teacher certification ratio	23.1%	25%	25%	UNC students as a percentage of all students recommended for teaching certification
14. Placement of graduates	93.8%	93.8%	93.8%	Percent of graduates employed or in advanced study one year after graduation
15. Instructional cost	$2,840	TBD	TBD	State general fund for instruction divided by student FTE
16. Funds generated by research corporation	$6.4 million	$10.3 million	$15 million	Total dollars generated by sponsored programs
17. Funds generated by UNC foundation	$1.8 million	$2.7 million	$4 million	Total dollars generated by annual giving
18. Institutional grant and scholarship aid per FTE	22.5%	25%	30%	Percentage of institutional aid of total aid
19. On-campus student support services cost	$683	TBD	TBD	Expenditures for student services divided by student FTE
20. Meeting authorized state appropriation	$30.7 million	TBD	TBD	Annual appropriated dollars from all sources

Unanimous agreement was reached that the current technological infrastructure was inadequate to position UNC students in the forefront of graduates in competition for scarce employment opportunities. A number of initiatives are underway including the completion of a new fiber optic backbone, the acquisition and implementation of a completely integrated administrative information system, and the redesign of the academic technology infrastructure to support global scholarship and alternative learning styles.

Availability of resources is key to implementing strategy. Strategies that emerged included tightening the model used to manage enrollments, ensuring that UNC met the strategic intent of recent legislation, refining services and increasing productivity per unit, developing new revenue sources, enhancing development activities, and monitoring service performance.

Illinois Benedictine College

Illinois Benedictine College (IBC) is a denominational college affiliated with St. Procopius Abbey and located in the western suburbs of Chicago, Illinois. Its undergraduate programs enroll 1,650 students, of whom about 600 live on campus. The pipeline for new undergraduate students is about equally divided between first-time and transfer students. The college serves many adult learners. Its major claim to undergraduate program distinction is its science programs, which have an excellent reputation for preparing students for medical school. Several years ago, IBC acquired the graduate programs of the failing George Williams College, and today its master's programs in business administration, counseling psychology, exercise physiology, management information systems, organizational behavior, and public health enroll 950 students. The college is located on a 100-acre campus in a pleasant, safe suburban setting.

The college engaged in a four-month strategic planning process orchestrated by one of the authors, using a variation of the SDE. The strategic planning team consisted of administrators, faculty, and students. One variation from the model was that the college also asked the consultant to develop a five-year financial model that would focus the impact of strategies on resource allocation and the overall financial health of the institution.

The planning team found that the college had significant strengths and weaknesses. Its location in the Chicago suburbs presented many advantages and opportunities. While IBC had experienced modest enrollment growth, it was experiencing ballooning student aid requirements and difficulties in maintaining the student profile it desired. Moreover, IBC was not in robust financial condition. Lacking a significant endowment, it had annually balanced its budgets, but at the expense of a large accumulated deferred maintenance balance. It lacked any real campus master plan, and had no vision for campus facilities and programs that might capture the imagination of faculty, students, donors, and the community. The campus also needed to find ways to unify around a shared purpose the various factions of the campus community. Strong leadership was required at all levels.

To achieve these ends, the planning team proceeded to develop a statement of strategic intent and mission; conduct an analysis of strengths, weaknesses, opportunities, and threats; and develop a set of KPIs. It then proceeded to craft strategies that were driven by the KPIs. The strategies fell into five groupings: leadership, physical facilities and infrastructure, financial resources, strategic enrollment management, and academic programs. To achieve these strategies, the planning team developed specific actions and objectives indicators by which they could measure the completion of the actions. They set annual targets for the KPIs out to five years from the baseline period.

Table 5.6 portrays the KPIs developed by Illinois Benedictine College to drive its strategies and decisions. The table presents the baseline values and the annual targets that were established. These KPIs include both quantitative and qualitative targets. The index column expresses the final year's (1998–1999) values as a proportion of the baseline year (1993–1994).

IBC chose a set of KPI drivers in eight categories: enrollment, student progress, quality of students, quality of programs, faculty, financial conditions, facilities, and campus and community life. The combination of these KPIs enabled the college to focus on different drivers for its undergraduate and graduate programs, develop a financial model for the health of the institution, and understand the interconnection between the different KPIs. This approach has led not only to the adoption of the strategies, actions, and indicators, but to the use of a financial resources model that enables members of the campus community to understand better the contributing factors to the programmatic and financial health of the campus.

Conclusion: KPIs Can Drive Strategic Decision Making

We have found that KPIs can drive strategic decision making in colleges and universities. To this end, we have successfully applied two levels of KPIs in the strategic planning process.

First, we have developed institutional-level KPIs that are the important, campus-wide measures of student quality and progress, institutional size, resources, and desired institutional outcomes. Most institutions develop twenty to thirty such KPIs. Strategies and initiatives are given higher priorities if they are judged to make more substantial contributions to achieving the targets established for the institution-level KPIs.

Second, there are program-level KPIs that deal with issues of program outcomes and quality. For some programs, this means customer service and meeting stakeholder needs. In these cases, the program must develop the capacity to answer a three-part question: What are the needs and wants of my customers or stakeholders? How successfully are we meeting those needs and wants? and What are the areas for improvement? The development of these measures typically is left to the individual programs, in collaboration with campus leadership. However, the program's leadership must be held accountable for achieving clearly identified targets for quality and satisfaction.

Table 5.6. Summary of KPIs for Illinois Benedictine College

KPI	1993–1994	1994–1995	1995–1996	1996–1997	1997–1998	1998–1999	Index
Enrollment							
FTE students	269	269	265	277	279	277	1.030
New transfers	241	241	242	235	242	234	0.971
Residential students	595	595	595	595	595	595	1.000
Undergraduate headcount	1,650	1,650	1,642	1,646	1,662	1,647	0.995
Undergraduate FTE	1,320	1,320	1,320	1,310	1,300	1,300	0.985
Minority student body (%)	10	11	12	13	14	15	1.500
Total graduate headcount	951	951	977	1,004	1,030	1,058	1.110
Graduate SCH	18,000	18,000	18,500	19,000	19,500	20,000	1.111
Graduate FTE	443.8	443.8	456.1	468.5	480.8	493.1	1.111
Student Progress							
Undergraduate fall-to-fall retention	85	85	86	86	87	87	1.024
Undergraduate five-year graduation rate	52	53	55	58	60	60	1.154
Graduate retention rate	TBD	TBD	TBD	TBD	TBD	TBD	TBD
Graduate graduation rate	TBD	TBD	TBD	TBD	TBD	TBD	TBD
Quality of Students							
Top high school quartile %	48	49	50	51	52	53	1.104
Average ACT score	22.7	22.8	22.9	23.0	23.1	23.2	1.022
Percent < minimum ACT	23	21	19	17	15	13	0.565
Percent over 28 ACT	9.7	10.0	10.5	11.0	11.5	12.0	1.237
Quality of Programs							
Program quality standards	TBD	TBD	TBD	TBD	TBD	TBD	TBD

Table 5.6. *(continued)*

KPI	1993–1994	1994–1995	1995–1996	1996–1997	1997–1998	1998–1999	Index
Faculty							
Percent minority	4	4	5	6	7	8	2.000
Student–faculty ratio	14	14	14	14	14	14	1.000
% Undergraduate SCH by PT faculty	22	22	22	20	20	20	0.909
Average graduate class size	18.5	19.0	19.5	20.0	20.0	20.0	1.081
Financial Conditions							
Annual philanthropic contributions (millions)	2.0	2.4	2.8	3.2	3.6	4.0	2.000
Value of endowment (millions)	7.437	TBD	TBD	TBD	TBD	TBD	TBD
True endowment (millions)	5.000	TBD	TBD	TBD	TBD	TBD	TBD
Funds balance (millions)	0.849	TBD	TBD	TBD	TBD	TBD	TBD
Contribution from academic programs (millions)	4.441	4.776	4.194	5.624	6.246	6.884	1.550
Tuition as % of revenue	74.8	74.8	74.8	74.7	74.6	74.5	0.996
Tuition discounting (%)	30	27	27	27	27	27	0.900
Deferred maintenance (millions)	20.0	20.0	19.5	18.5	17.5	16.5	0.825
Facilities							
Facilities quality index	TBD	TBD	TBD	TBD	TBD	TBD	TBD
Campus/Community Life							
Campus life quality index	TBD	TBD	TBD	TBD	TBD	TBD	TBD

The SDE easily accommodates reengineering, continuous quality improvement (CQI), and other tools of transformation, either as independent strategies or as integral parts of other strategies. KPIs are an integral component of reengineering and CQI initiatives. As colleges and universities confront the need to realign themselves to dramatically changing environments and stakeholder expectations, they will come to appreciate the utility of KPIs as drivers of decision making and an essential element of transformation.

MICHAEL G. DOLENCE is strategic planning administrator at California State University, Los Angeles, and a management consultant who has served as a principal on a variety of projects for Strategic Initiatives, Inc.

DONALD M. NORRIS is president of Strategic Initiatives, Inc. a management consulting firm located in Herndon, Virginia.

*An economic model is described for evaluating the cost perfor-
mance of academic and administrative programs. Examples from
one university show how the model has been used to control costs
and reengineer processes.*

Activity-Based Costing Model for Assessing Economic Performance

Daniel W. DeHayes, Joseph G. Lovrinic

Many institutions of higher education are confronting opposing pressures to increase performance while reducing costs, or at least holding the line on them. Thus, cost containment has received considerable attention in the literature of higher education over the last several years, as epitomized by the works of Robert Zemsky and William Massy (1990). In addition, many institutions are examining their methods and performance with regard to obtaining and allocating resources. This chapter will examine how Indiana University–Purdue University Indianapolis designed and developed activity-based costing tools to address these pressures. It will also describe how those tools were applied within schools and service units to assess costs of campus-level outputs (students, research projects), measure the economic performance of existing academic and service processes, and set benchmarks for reengineering those processes.

Although cost issues have been a recent topic in the higher education literature, it has not always been so. Leslie and Brinkman (1988), in their book *The Economic Value of Higher Education,* note that the term *economics of education* was first used in 1960. By 1972, a few economists were specializing in this field and becoming influential in federal and state education policy making. The topic appeared as an item for discussion on morning news programs. As more pressing national and state economic needs emerged, public resources allocated to higher education came under even greater scrutiny. Although perhaps not reduced in public favor, higher education saw its support diminish as health care, care for the aged, and penal system demands increased. As Beatty (1977) notes, the importance of cost information increases as resources diminish, thereby driving the legislatures' demands for accountability for their investment in higher education.

NEW DIRECTIONS FOR INSTITUTIONAL RESEARCH, no. 82, Summer 1994   © Jossey-Bass Publishers

As calls for cost information increased, cost models were seen as a way of gathering cost information and creating a means of addressing what-if questions regarding shifts of resources and adjustments to cost structures. Among these was the resource requirements prediction model developed by the National Center for Higher Education Management Systems (1973). This was essentially a mainframe computer-based system using institutional data bases, capable of analyzing various alternatives for resource use. It also included analysis of productivity ratios.

Cost and productivity measures have long been recognized as key performance indicators in the academic community. Industry, as well as government and nonprofit institutions, had for some time faced the same issues, and each had developed its own set of techniques for assembling meaningful data for use in effective decision making. During the 1980s, standard cost accounting was no longer considered effective in all situations, given the changes that had taken place in the economic environment and the types of issues that were being faced. As a result, a new methodology evolved that focused on analysis of production activities. It is appropriately named *activity-based costing.* Some analysts thought this new methodology might likewise be of benefit in the complex cost environment of higher education. Turk, in his 1992 article, "The ABCs of Activity-Based Costing," suggested ways in which this approach could be applied.

Activity-based costing provides a method to trace financial inputs through various production activities (such as classroom instruction and laboratory usage) to the variety of instructional, research, and service outputs of higher education.

Costs are but one aspect of institutional performance, one that underpins virtually all institutional functions. Although costs cannot stand alone as performance indicators, the cost component of performance must be assessed in order to fully judge the value added by various educational processes.

The application of activity-based costing methodologies has been studied at Indiana University during the last few years, with the goal of developing a method to assess the economic aspects of a campus. It has been generally called the economic model. This model was conceived initially as a tool to assist campus administrators who had recently moved to a responsibility center management (RCM) environment (Whalen, 1991). RCM gives school deans far more authority to manage their revenues and budget allocations than do more traditional budgeting techniques. RCM was adopted to tie financial management more closely to academic management. The RCM environment provides the organizational context for using activity-based costing as a means of assessing the cost component of school performance.

Indiana University Experience

Like many of its peers in higher education, Indiana University is facing the challenge of increasing costs and diminishing state support. Having recently implemented RCM, which gave deans the authority to collect and distribute their own financial resources, the university leadership realized that more was needed than simply conferring this authority. The deans needed to know how the distribution of resources could best be accomplished—that is, from which areas of their schools' budgets could funds be recovered, and to which areas those funds should be reallocated. There was also some agreement that current budgeting processes portray the cost of inputs, such as personnel, rather than the cost of outputs, such as degree programs. This difference causes a fundamental disconnection between how academic administration thinks about its future in output terms and the information it receives on costs.

Accordingly, a methodology to examine the economic performance of a campus was conceived in late 1990, to be used as a tool to assist campus administrators and deans in fulfilling their new duties within the RCM environment. Once the allocation of resources was delegated to operational levels, it became necessary for resource managers to understand fully the costs of their operations and the impact of their reallocation decisions. Initial steps in defining the theory of the model began in January 1991.

Later that year, the Indiana University–Purdue University Indianapolis (IUPUI) campus, one of eight in the Indiana University system, volunteered to be the prototype site for the economic model effort. A team drawn from the schools of dentistry and business, together with the campus' accounting office, met with an internal consulting group to develop economic models of two of the Indianapolis campus outputs: the B.S. degree graduate in business, and the D.D.S. degree graduate in dentistry.

IUPUI was particularly receptive to both the implementation of RCM and the development of economic modeling. A comparatively new campus (in existence since 1969), it has more than 27,000 students and 1,400 full-time faculty and offers diverse degree programs in nineteen schools. IUPUI is a joint venture between Indiana University and Purdue University, with Indiana University serving as the managing partner. Through its programs, IUPUI is helping define a new type of American urban university that excels in research—IUPUI generated nearly $90 million in external support in 1992–1993—while offering a full range of educational programs from associate degrees and college preparatory study through doctoral and professional degrees. The campus has based its future on continuous program evaluation, innovative programming, and careful resource management.

Using activity-based costing techniques, the team developed the basic mechanics of the model, implementing the model using conventional spreadsheet tools on a desktop computer. The models were seen as viable tools for analyzing operations and costs and for creating scenarios of various alternative resource allocation decisions. The campus leadership decided to expand the model effort further during the 1992–1993 school year to include further detail within the school of dentistry and to include the planning office and integrated technologies support unit. For the 1993–1994 school year, the economic model effort is broadening to more areas of the IUPUI campus, including additional schools and academic departments in the school of science, other campus support offices, and cross-departmental processes.

Economic Model

The economic model consists of the following elements:

A graphic view of interrelated organizations that depicts the outputs produced by academic units and the services produced by support units that are then consumed by academic units

An activity-based costing matrix that defines the costs of various outputs and allows what-if cost analyses in response to variations in certain input parameters

A work flow analysis that can assist the organization in enhancing its current activities through a detailed review and reengineering of the tasks involved in those activities

As a management tool designed to assist unit administrators in their understanding of operations within an economic perspective, the model can help deans and directors optimize their resource allocation decisions. It can also be a key component in successfully realizing the benefits of RCM. The value of the model can be especially significant when resources must be reallocated during periods of constrained funding.

In short, the model is specifically designed to enable units to determine more complete and accurate cost performance measures for costing the unit's products, identify restructuring opportunities, and estimate the impact of proposed changes in operations and varying customer demand. In addition, the model has four peripheral benefits: development of a collective understanding of how each unit contributes to the outputs of the campus (instruction, research, and service), more precise illustration of the interdependencies among units in fulfillment of their missions; broadened management understanding of unit-level operations; and establishment of a foundation for reengineering operations and applying total quality management through development of costing benchmarks for continuous improvement efforts.

Concept of an Economic Model. The economic model seeks to trace the flow of product outputs or services from suppliers through an organizational unit to the final delivery of instruction, research, and service products to the university's constituents. Specific attention is given to identifying the flow of information among units. Such tracing helps identify the resource impact of, for instance, the addition of a new major in school A on the class load of prerequisite courses offered by school B, as well as the increase in effort required of the registrar's office. As such, the model is useful as a planning tool, especially for what-if scenario analysis.

Besides identifying the linkages among units, the model forms the basis for detailed analysis of the activities required to produce each output and their costs. In this mode, the model seeks to identify the direct cost of various outputs from the unit so that rational pricing (or acknowledged subsidization) decisions can be implemented. The activity analysis involved in this phase can also identify slack resources and opportunities for enhancement of operations through organizational, procedural, or technological change.

Steps in Building an Economic Model. The three principal stages involved in the model building process are listed below. Within each is a simplified description of the various component tasks.

Define the model.

 Determine the scope of the model; that is, which organizational units will need to be included in order to get a reasonable picture of the outputs to be examined?

 Identify all the outputs of the units being studied and establish a working dialogue with experts in each of those units who know the process required to produce each output.

 Draw a diagram of the overall process flow for the outputs being examined (see Figure 6.1). Note that Figure 6.1 is at a very high level of aggregation; that is, many tasks are captured in each of the ovals. The effectiveness of the model is enhanced significantly when the process or activity analysis is developed at a detailed level for activities that add significant cost. For example, in studying the B.S. in business administration degree, more than 250 separate tasks were identified and costed.

**Figure 6.1. Product Output Analysis (Process Flow)
for Producing a Graduate**

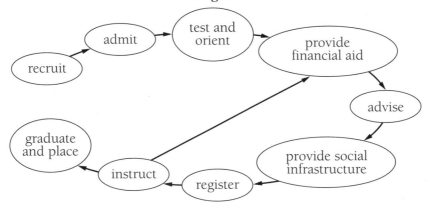

Gather the data.
> Define the tasks associated with each activity and their frequencies for each organizational unit in the process flow for each product.
>
> Identify the individuals performing each task within the specified organizational units.
>
> Determine the hours that each individual (or labor group) gives to each occurrence of the task.
>
> Determine the cost factors that apply to each individual or labor group or that apply directly to the output. Cost includes not only salary but also all benefits.

Assemble data into the model matrix.
> Calculate the average cost per hour for each labor group (for example, mid-level professional).
>
> Calculate total hours per labor group per task.
>
> Multiply those hours by the corresponding average hourly cost to get the cost per labor group task.
>
> Add the labor group costs within task to get cost per task.
>
> Divide by the number of outputs to determine the cost per task per output.
>
> Add the task costs within activity to determine cost per activity per output.
>
> Multiply the activity costs by their frequencies to determine cost per activity per final output.
>
> Add the costs per activity per final output to already allocated output costs to determine total cost per final output.

Clearly, many calculations are necessary to "roll up" the cost of the output from the detailed information collected on each significant task involved in the process. However, with today's computer tools, the calculation chores are relatively simple. The critical factor that limits the quality of the modeling effort is the quality of the data base collected on the time to be complete the critical tasks and the specification of the component parts of each process.

The Model Matrix. The matrix is a series of linked spreadsheets that contains the interconnection of data described above. These data are loaded into various levels of the matrix:

Level 1. Activities that make up the production process for each output
Level 2. Tasks that make up the activities listed in level 1
Level 3. Labor hour allocation per task listed in level 2
Level 4. Cost components of faculty and staff labor identified in level 3

The linkage among the spreadsheets allows the detailed cost and task data collected at the detail level (3 and 4) to "bubble up" to the ultimate cost of the final output (level 1). It also makes possible changes to any component item (hours, task, cost) and provides a view of the overall effect on final cost.

Limitations of the Model. Although the model can be a very versatile tool, its application is constrained in several ways. The client's queries of the model must relate only to the activities, tasks, labor groups, and labor costs contained in the model. In other words, questions outside the scope of the model cannot be answered with model data.

The quality of the data collection effort determines the quality of the output. However, regardless of how careful one is in collecting time effort data, the values collected are only estimates. As such, extreme care must be taken to not use the output in too precise a form. That is, the cost estimates for degrees should not be considered accurate to the dollar level, but should be used more in comparison to the costs of other school outputs.

Quality measures can explicitly be built into the model only if they are defined using quantifiable values. For example, assuming that class size affects instructional quality, an average class size could be used as a qualitative measure.

The model is not constructed using an optimization methodology, and therefore cannot provide any optimal answers. For example, the model cannot answer such questions as "What is the optimal number of graduates for the B.S. in business program?" It can, however, provide a series of alternatives by working through a series of what-if questions.

The user of the model must still interpret the findings provided by the model—the model itself does not direct a course of action.

Applications of the Economic Model

Over the past three years, the economic model has been applied within several academic and administrative units at IUPUI. These efforts have included costing of the instructional outputs of academic units and service delivery programs within campus administrative units.

In the prototype model development effort at IUPUI, two significant outputs were selected for analysis: the B.S. degree from the school of business and the D.D.S. degree from the school of dentistry. These outputs were chosen because they represented the greatest single portion of total output within their schools. To limit the scope of the prototype effort to a manageable size, five key support units were selected for analysis: bursar, admissions, registrar, financial aid, and facility services. These five support units provide significant support for the production of the selected degrees. Other support units (such as the library and integrated technologies) also provide significant effort in allowing schools to produce degrees recipients, but the prototyping effort was designed only to demonstrate feasibility. All other support units were analyzed in later efforts. While the feasibility of the model was demonstrated, a key concern of the developers was the impact it could have on current deliberations in these administrative and academic organizations.

Several applications of model results as performance indicators were considered. First, the model could be used to estimate the total cost of a particular administrative operation in comparison to the cost of outsourcing that service. Second, the model could refine the cost estimate of particular degrees in determining fee structure. Third, the output from the model could be used to assist unit leadership in restructuring operations based in part on much more complete and accurate cost information. The final application was selected to demonstrate the ultimate value of the model in university operations.

Restructuring Operations Using Output Cost Information. A professional school agreed to apply the model to its strategic planning process, which was already under way. The school's leadership enthusiastically embraced the model in order to understand more about the costs of the school's outputs. Although a great deal was known about the cost of inputs to its operation (such as personnel, facilities maintenance, and information technology infrastructure), little was known about the exact cost of all the outputs (instruction, research, and service), or where people were spending their time in order to identify how effort and costs could be reallocated.

The school enjoyed an excellent national reputation, but its financial situation was not as positive. By the latest estimates, the budget deficit through the end of the decade would range between $650,000 and $2,500,000 and several important items were not budgeted (such as a badly needed building renovation and significant improvement of the electronic infrastructure). The total financial shortfall was estimated by the dean at more than $4 million by the end of the decade (the annual budget of unrestricted funds totaled about $19 million). In addition, the budget estimates did not provide for more than nominal salary increases and little expansion of the supplies and expenses allowance.

Clearly, something had to be done. But without good cost information, it was not clear what to do. Under these circumstances, it was likely that significant across-the-board budget cuts would result. (In the past, the school had resorted to such cuts, only to enter into a downward spiral in funding, morale, and quality of programs.) It was also possible that the school could resort to another frequently mentioned budget cutting strategy—to cut programs that were not top quality. Although this sounded like a useful strategy, it is often too difficult to draw a dividing line on quality when accurate estimates of cost of the various programs are not known. In such a capital-rationing scenario, not only are the quality and amount of outputs critical to measure performance, but the cost to generate each of those outputs is important to understand as well.

Application of the model began with adjusting the planning process to include a specific step where cost data for each output could be collected and reviewed. Note that this addition meant that the unit wanted to assess not only the quality of its outputs, but also the cost of its outputs.

Once the planning group had accepted the notion of assessing cost as well as quality of each of its outputs, the process of applying the economic model could begin. The first step was to work with the leadership of the school to identify all of the major outputs and the time applied to each output by the faculty and staff in the school. The following twenty outputs were identified, including six teaching outputs, four research outputs, and ten service outputs (other activities—not outputs—included administration, vacation and other time off, and committee work not directly associated with an output):

Teaching
    Vocational education
      One-year program
      Two-year program
    Undergraduate education
    Graduate education
      Two-year programs
      Three-year programs
      Four-year programs
Research
    Sponsored
      Commercial
      Federal
      Other
    Nonsponsored
Service
    Outreach programs
    Professional practice
    Professional organizations
    Departmental laboratory
      Internal
      External
    Continuing education
      Internal
      External
    Consulting
      Within the school
      With other schools at IU
      External to IU

Once agreement was reached on the list of outputs, each output was analyzed in terms of how it should be measured and how exactly the output is produced. For example, the steps necessary to prepare and conduct a course were studied in order to guide later time or effort data-collection efforts. This detailed activity analysis was also useful in identifying which support units assist in the production of each output and exactly how they contribute. An example of a high-level activity analysis is shown in Figure 6.1. This figure shows the basic steps needed to create an instructional output of the school. Each oval in the figure was further analyzed in detail, creating a long list of steps and the organizations involved in the process. Although detailed activity analysis is applicable in many instances, some outputs cannot be analyzed in such a structured manner. For example, it is very difficult to list the exact steps in the creative process of research. However, the analysis team found that the basic steps could be listed for all outputs and the organizations involved in each production process could be identified.

After the activity analysis was completed, effort data were collected (where feasible and practical) for each of the personnel categories that spent time on each output. Personnel in the school and in other academic or administrative support units were included in the data collection process. The list of steps discovered in the activity analysis was used to prompt people to remember all the steps needed to produce an output. At the request of the planning group, the data on the teaching outputs were collected at the course level. In this way, the total cost to conduct each course was calculated.

In order to complete the total cost estimate, both school and campus budgets were searched for nonpersonnel costs that applied to this school. As is true in most organizations, some costs are managed centrally (such as utilities and facility replacement). In order to develop a true picture of the total cost to produce the school's outputs, these additional figures were considered necessary.

Two reports were created for the school's leadership to use in their planning deliberations. First, the total cost to conduct each course in the school was estimated. Second, the total cost for each of the twenty major outputs was estimated. Table 6.1 shows a portion of the total-cost-by-output report. For each of the twenty outputs (identified as rows in the table), the total attributable cost is shown. For this table, total cost was calculated as the sum of salary and benefits of personnel in the school, budgeted nonpersonnel costs, the costs in support units whose services are purchased by the school, and costs that are managed centrally or not currently budgeted by the school and are therefore hidden.

Analysis of the data in Table 6.1 revealed some interesting findings:

The total cost of the school (including all costs incurred anywhere in the institution) totaled $26,411,000—considerably more than the $19,000,000 budget of the school.

More than 46 percent of the cost of the school was consumed by its teaching function. Another 23 percent ($6.038 million) was consumed in research, and 11 percent of the cost went to service activities. The remainder of the cost was attributable to overhead.

More than 27 percent of the total cost of the school went to activities that generated no revenue. Everyone in the school was surprised that the time and money spent on these activities was that high. To be sure, many of these activities are important (including a variety of service activities), but this

Table 6.1. Total School Cost by Output

Instruction	Product	Total Attributable Cost (000's)
Vocational Education	One-year program	$170
	Two-year program	$769
Undergraduate Education	four year program	$6,487
Graduate Education	Two-year programs	$1,769
	Three-year programs	$1,846
	Four-year programs	$1,077
Total: Instruction		$12,119
Service		
	Outreach programs	$85
	Professional practice	$1,260
	Professional organization	$243
Departmental laboratory	Internal	$75
	External	$738
Continuing education	Internal	$52
	External	$175
Consulting	Within the school	$113
	Other schools at IU	$34
	External to IU	$129
Total: Service		$2,904
Research		
Sponsored	Commercial	$2,167
	Federal	$817
	Other	$1,935
Nonsponsored	Activity	$1,119
Total: Research		$6,038
Overhead		
Administration	School/departmental time	$2,336
Committee commitments	School	$349
	Campus/university	$81
Unassigned hours	Vacation/holidays	$170
	Professional development	$432
	Other (specify)	$202
Miscellaneous	Unassigned RCB allocations	$1,474
	Unassigned equipment depreciation	$307
Total: Overhead		$5,351
Total School Cost		$26,411

cost was worrisome. Further analysis found that much of that cost was attributed to high administrative costs. As a result, the school cut the number of academic departments from sixteen to six and reduced the size of the dean's office.

A large variance was found in the number of hours required to teach seemingly comparable courses. This finding prompted the planning group to investigate the reasons for the variance further so as to address some of the possible quality and cost problems.

Some of the graduate programs were found to cost more than three times the value received from student fees and student work activities in the school.

These and a number of other findings about the cost structure of the school were then used by the planning group to design a set of twelve initiatives intended to correct the projected $4 million financial deficit in the school while maintaining teaching and research quality. These initiatives expanded programs where the cost–benefit ratio demonstrated positive opportunities and cut costs where current experience was clearly out of line with what is needed. Across-the-board cuts have not been needed.

Summary

The economic model starts by examining the interrelationships among a college's or university's organizational units and the product outputs and services shared among them. It uses an activity-based costing matrix to define cost performance measures for various outputs and allow what-if analyses of cost variations. It may also include work-flow analysis that can assist an organization in enhancing its activities through a detailed review and reengineering of the tasks involved in those activities.

The situation in which universities often find themselves clearly suggests that capital rationing will be needed for years to come. In such instances, up-to-date data on critical output performance indicators are essential. But in such rationing situations, data on output quantity and quality alone are insufficient. That is, it is not sufficient to know that a school has achieved some output level or quality. Academic leaders must focus on the cost to achieve such levels of output as another aspect of performance. For example, it is useful to understand the cost to produce graduates who report satisfaction at the 80 percent level. Today's focus on performance improvement means that academic leaders need to understand more than just the current level of student satisfaction. They also need to know what the cost would be to raise that level to 90 percent through, for example, reducing section sizes or having more senior faculty teach lower-division courses.

Cost performance indicators can also be used in comparisons with other institutions. The cost to produce a graduate of comparable quality levels (measured by board scores or placement records or other measures) at university A versus university B is becoming a critical arguing point in the reallocation of scarce resources. Although such efficiency measures should not determine resource allocations, history has shown in almost every other institution that the ability to achieve outputs at the lowest cost attracts additional financial resources. Adding more accurate cost data to the list of performance indicators measured by an academic institution is where the economic model discussed here can be of value.

References

Beatty, G., Jr. "The Application of Costing Methodologies in Higher Education." In D. Hopkins and R. Schroeder (eds.), *Applying Analytical Methods to Planning and Management.* New Directions for Institutional Research, no. 13. San Francisco: Jossey-Bass, 1977.

Leslie, L. L., and Brinkman, P. T. *The Economic Value of Higher Education.* New York: American Council on Education and Macmillan Publishing Company, 1988.

National Center for Higher Education Management Systems. *Introduction to the Resource Requirements Prediction Model.* National Center for Higher Education Management Systems at the Western Interstate Commission for Higher Education tech report 34a, 1973.

Turk, F. J. "The ABCs of Activity-Based Costing." *NACUBO Business Officer,* 1992, 7, 36–43.

Whalen, E. L. *Responsibility Center Budgeting.* Bloomington, Ind.: Indiana University Press, 1991.

Zemsky, R., and Massy, W. F. "Cost Containment: Committing to a New Economic Reality." *Change,* 1990, 22 (6), 16–22.

DANIEL W. DEHAYES is professor of business administration and director of the Center for Entrepreneurship and Innovation, Indiana University Graduate School of Business.

JOSEPH G. LOVRINIC is management advisor to the vice president for planning and finance management, Indiana University.

Performance indicators can be developed at any level of academic administration, but the college or university level is the optimal starting point. This chapter describes five standards for developing PIs that will guide strategic decision making.

Performance Indicators for Accountability and Improvement

Trudy W. Banta, Victor M. H. Borden

"What business are you in?" barked W. Edwards Deming in his deep, raspy monotone. "Who are your customers? What do they need and want? What does that say about what you're trying to accomplish? How will you know you've been successful?" Deming was relentless in his questioning, always pushing his listeners to examine their own purposes, methods, and outcomes. In his last decade of life, W. Edwards Deming was finally recognized widely in his own country as the premiere exponent of continuous improvement of methods and thus outcomes, and was pursued by the best minds in virtually every field. All who were introduced to him hoped to hear some pearl of wisdom that would help them achieve their aspirations for excellence. But he provided few answers. Instead, his listeners were most often confronted by questions; like Socrates, Deming sought to draw truth from deep within individuals. Both philosophers understood that we learn best when encouraged to look within our own experience, organize our thoughts, apply our hypotheses, and see whether they work.

Regardless of how one views Deming's work and the myriad interpretations manifesting themselves as "total quality management"—a term with which Deming himself did not like to be associated—his questions remain fundamental. In providing our own responses, we confer purpose upon our actions and thus upon our search for indications of successful accomplishment.

Performance indicators (PIs) derive their significance from their ability to link outcomes both with purposes and with processes. When used correctly, PIs can be an essential element in addressing Deming's basic questions. With this tribute to Deming's perspicacity and intellectual leadership, in this final chapter we articulate a set of standards that may be helpful to those who must select or develop performance indicators for use on their own campuses. Whereas Ewell and Jones in Chapter Two have offered some properties that apply particularly to state-level indicators, the emphasis here is on the institution, where improvements are most likely to be made. The suggested criteria will be illustrated with examples from our own experience and from that reported by other contributors to this volume.

Standards for Performance Indicators

The standards or criteria we propose for judging performance indicators (PIs) may be stated quite simply. We admit at the outset we are being idealistic; few if any existing PI systems meet all these criteria. Nevertheless, we believe that PIs should have a clear purpose, be coordinated throughout an organization or system (vertical alignment), extend across the entire range of organizational processes (horizontal alignment), be derived from a variety of coordinated methods, and be used to inform decision making.

Purpose of PIs. A clear purpose is essential to the success of a system of performance indicators. How will the indicators be used? Many external agencies responsible for funding higher education seem more interested in outcomes and in PIs as means of demonstrating that colleges and universities are using their resources wisely, whereas faculty and campus administrators are most supportive of outcomes assessment and other data-collection efforts that will help them improve teaching and learning, the overall student experience, and administrative processes. To date, outcomes assessment that has taken place on campuses for the purpose of demonstrating institutional accountability has produced little information that external decision makers find helpful or satisfying. Although there is a growing body of evidence that conscientiously implemented improvement-oriented assessment activities are helping faculty improve educational programs (Banta and Associates, 1993), there is a clear need for academics to address decision makers' needs for accountability data if the provision of resources to support those improved programs is to continue in the future.

Saying that an indicator system needs a clear purpose sounds relatively straightforward, but it may be the most difficult of our five standards to achieve, especially in higher education where tradition dictates that scholars work alone in increasingly narrow disciplinary specialties. Few academics are adept at writing clear goals and most as yet see no reason for coming together with colleagues to develop common goals for curricula and for academic support programs.

The inability of academics and governmental representatives in Europe to agree on purpose and content for indicators has made indicator systems there relatively impotent. The accountability mechanisms suggested by governments have been shown by academics to be flawed, but academics have not been able to identify indicators that would satisfy the twin purposes of accountability and improvement. In Chapter Three, Jongbloed and Westerheijden illustrate how the lack of common purpose has undermined the development of national PIs in several European countries. As a result, current quality assurance efforts are considered distinct from PI development. For the time being, the institutions have won more autonomy—more flexibility in managing their own affairs—but the accountability questions remain on the table. There is a clear implication that institutions must find ways to address these questions or risk the loss of government funds.

Though starting in very different places vis-à-vis government control of higher education, the U.S. and European situations in the last decade have rapidly come to resemble each other closely. Unlike their European counterparts, U.S. colleges and universities historically have functioned with very little state or federal interference. But with the increasing need to spread scarce resources over a variety of services, more questions about the relative contribution to society of higher education versus highways, prisons, and public schools have had to be answered. If U.S. colleges and universities object to campus crime statistics, dropout percentages, and loan default rates as performance indicators, they must negotiate the right to supply other measures. As in Europe, the time for doing so is growing short. In statehouses across the country, it is becoming more and more difficult to convince lawmakers of the need for continuing increases in funding for higher education.

Several of this volume's authors have participated during the last three years in the U.S. debate over national goals and indicators of performance for higher education (Ewell and Jones, 1993; Banta, 1993). Time and time again, the question of purpose for an indicator system has been raised. The Task Force on Assessing the National Goal Relating to Postsecondary Education (1992) has stated its intention to establish an accountability mechanism; spokespersons for higher education have called this short-sighted and argued for a system that would promote improvement (Jones, 1994). Partly because of this stalemate over purpose, there is at least a temporary hiatus with respect to developing this system.

In Tennessee, where the desire to base funding decisions in part on some qualitative indicators led the Tennessee Higher Education Commission (THEC) to initiate performance funding in 1979 (Banta, 1988), the purpose question (assessment for accountability or improvement) was raised continually by institutional representatives until 1992. With the adoption of its third five-year plan for performance funding, the THEC added a statement of purpose to its guidelines that espoused both accountability and improvement (Tennessee Higher Education Commission, 1992). Moreover, in moving from five to ten performance funding standards, the THEC added several criteria that reward institutions for improvement against their own benchmarks on locally developed goals.

It should be emphasized that everyone wants colleges and universities to improve. Even external bodies that use accountability as the fundamental purpose for PIs hope that the indicator system will ultimately improve higher education. However, the debate quickly becomes politically charged and neither side seems capable of identifying or developing indicators that serve both purposes simultaneously.

No matter how difficult or painful the process of coming to agreement, the involvement of decision makers is vital to the ultimate success of an indicator system. Indicators that are not used obviously have no meaning or value. Ultimate utility is much more likely if those charged with making decisions specify initially the kinds of data they will consider credible and helpful.

This discussion suggests two kinds of purposes: the purpose for developing a PI system and the purpose of the institution—its mission and goals. We believe that these purposes should be mutually supportive in order for PI development to serve both accountability and improvement. PIs are most usefully developed as a means to define institutional mission and goals operationally and to monitor progress toward their achievement. As we said at the outset, purpose is everything. All other standards for PIs follow sensibly once purpose is defined.

Aligning PIs Throughout the Organization or System. Ideally, this country would have broad purposes for postsecondary education that attract a high degree of consensus among academics as well as the populace at large. Within this framework, states would develop purposes for their own systems that would support the national goals. Institutions within a state might then develop very different missions, but as Ewell and Jones have suggested in their chapter for this volume, the overall aims of a state system of higher education can be accomplished if component institutions contribute differently to overall state purposes in their own specialized areas of competence.

Within a given institution, constituent colleges or schools should have goals that contribute to the institutional mission, and departments or other units that make up each college or school should likewise have goals that complement those of their schools and of the institution. Although such unity of purpose is rare indeed in larger institutions, it may be found in a few smaller ones. Alverno College in Milwaukee and King's College in Wilkes-Barre, Pennsylvania are two such places.

Faculty at both have agreed-upon goals for student learning, all of which are addressed explicitly in every major and some of which are the focus of instruction in every course. At Alverno, the improvement of eight defined student abilities guides virtually all faculty and student effort: communication, analysis, problem solving, valuing in decision making, interacting, global perspectives, effective citizenship, and aesthetic responsiveness (Loacker and Mentkowski, 1993). At King's College, the eight transferable skills of liberal learning that shape the instructional program are critical thinking, problem solving, effective writing, effective oral communication, quantitative analysis, computer literacy, library and information technology competence, and values awareness (Farmer, 1988).

At Samford University in Birmingham, Alabama and Midlands Technical College in Columbia, South Carolina, planners have defined a small number of critical processes that are considered essential to institutional success. Samford's processes are enrollment management, fundraising, planning, faculty and staff hiring and management, learning, environment management, marketing, and compliance with regulations and standards (John Harris, personal communication, September 1992). The areas considered critical to the operation of Midlands Tech include accessible, comprehensive programs of high quality; student satisfaction and retention; posteducation satisfaction and success; economic development and community involvement; effective resource management; and dynamic organizational involvement and development. Samford has a series of performance measures that are drawn periodically at "strategic points" in each process to monitor how well the process is functioning. Midlands Tech regularly collects data on twenty indicators of effectiveness such as student knowledge and skills acquired in the major area of study, survey responses from employers and receiving institutions on the success of employees or transfer students, and student perceptions of the role of the college in achievement of their personal and career goals (Dorcus Kitchings, personal communication, November 1993).

Aligning PIs Across Inputs, Processes, and Outcomes. Input or resource indicators originally received most attention because they were easiest to measure. Doctoral level program reviews initiated in the United States in the 1970s focused on such resources as size of library collection, percentage of faculty with doctorates, and ability levels of incoming students (Richards and Minkel, 1986).

The 1980s saw a groundswell of interest in the other side of the ledger: outcomes. Following the advent of performance funding in Tennessee, which specified that institutions would gather detailed information about student achievement in general education and their majors, alumni satisfaction, and placement of graduates, three-quarters of the states adopted policies that caused public colleges and universities to collect and report some kind of outcome information.

More recently, Deming and others have caused us to turn our attention to the intervening processes that use resources to produce outcomes. Measuring an outcome will not, in and of itself, result in improvement, they say. We need to examine carefully the processes that lead to outcomes if we hope to improve them (see Chapter Four). The appendix contains examples of resource, process, and outcome indicators for each of several categories of concern to educators.

In Chapter Two, Ewell and Jones write that state-level indicators should provide policy leverage. They should not only be able to indicate the presence of a problem, but should also suggest how to correct it. This illustrates the link between outcomes and processes called for by Borden and Bottrill in Chapter One. For example, an institution may wish to increase the representation of minority groups in its student population. Monitoring the percentages of minority students over time would indicate the success or failure of meeting this objective, but any changes noted could not necessarily be attributed to actions taken by the institution. Even if the institution monitors regional demographics to see whether input conditions are changing, any shifts in outcomes might be attributable to actions of other institutions as well as one's own. On the other hand, if the institution sponsors a program of minority faculty speakers at local high schools, then compares the enrollment of minorities from those high schools with that from similar high schools where no special efforts were made, the selected PI will more likely indicate how well the special program works in increasing minority participation. This type of information, along with student perception data, would inform the decision to eliminate, expand, or improve the faculty speakers programs as a process designed to improve the institutional goal of increased minority participation.

The activity-based costing procedure described by DeHayes and Lovrinic in Chapter Six provides another example of linking indicators across the range of inputs, process, and outcomes. In their model, each product of a program is dissected into its task components, their interrelationships, and costs or inputs required. From this information, one can readily identify targets for improvement or reengineering: the areas that add the least value to the product relative to their cost. It was precisely this kind of information that led one of Indiana University's professional schools to consolidate its sixteen academic departments into six, thus saving administrative overhead that did not contribute significantly to the production of graduates.

In Chapter Four, Dooris and Teeter describe how faculty in the physics department at The Pennsylvania State University selected a range of indicators covering both processes and outcomes to guide their efforts to improve student learning among undergraduate engineering majors. The indicators included time students spend studying, student satisfaction with the introductory course, results of standardized tests of subject matter knowledge, and amount of out-of-class contact with instructors. The faculty are thus able to assess how their curricula and programs affect the full range of goals for student learning as they observe changes in the corresponding indicators.

Finally, it is important to point out that the input–process–output continuum has been conceptualized differently by some practitioners. Astin (1991), for instance, posits instead an input–environment–outcomes model. The Special Study Panel on Education Indicators went even further and rejected the input–process–outcome model as too simplistic, suggesting instead a more conceptually complex "pyramid of indicators" (Special Study Panel on Education Indicators, 1991, p. 43). At the base of the pyramid are selected statistics, findings, and profiles derived from data collection; at the center are clusters of indicators; at the top are a few composite indicators.

Coordinating a Variety of Methods. Many roads lead to Rome. There is no best method for encouraging a department or institution to consider its purpose, goals, processes, and outcomes. Some, such as Alverno and King's College, started by defining student learning outcomes, then developed instructional processes to promote the outcomes and performance indicators to chart student progress.

Faculty and administrators at Winona State University in Minnesota have developed a quality assurance and assessment plan with 250 indicators for monitoring achievements (Dennis Martin, personal communication, January 1994). The indicators, many of which are based on the "Seven Principles for Good Practice in Undergraduate Education" (Chickering and Gamson, 1987), address the institutional context and use of resources, curriculum and class structure and requirements, teaching practice, and student behavior (Ewell, 1990). Sources of data include surveys for first-year students, continuing students, graduating seniors, and faculty; demographic and other profile information collected in the admissions process; student performance as measured by faculty in classes; and library use statistics (Martin, 1994).

Some institutions, such as Ohio University (Williford and Moden, 1993) and the IUPUI schools of nursing and of engineering and technology have dynamic leaders who take personal charge of a strategic planning initiative that yields goal statements for all aspects of the unit's activities. Later it becomes clear to all concerned that indicators of effectiveness are needed to link plans, processes, and outcomes, thus closing the planning loop.

Several Indiana University professional schools have used the DeHayes–Lovrinic economic model described in this volume to study their fundamental processes. The findings have prompted an interest in PIs other than costs as the name of the planning game has become cost reduction.

In Chapter Five of this volume, Dolence and Norris describe a model they call the strategic decision engine, which uses key performance indicators and several group-oriented decision-making methodologies to drive the strategic planning process. Their examples from the University of Northern Colorado and Illinois Benedictine College show how those two institutions were able to focus institutional energy on several strategic processes and monitor performance via key performance indicators.

Some institutions undertake a study of TQM and discover the Shewhart (1939) plan–do–check–act cycle. This study can lead to the realization that carefully chosen PIs are essential in the check phase. McLaughlin and Snyder (1993) describe the application of the plan–do–check–act cycle to the institutional research function. They describe a range of indicators that can be used to monitor the effectiveness of IR functions at the office, program, and activity levels. Their indicators include time-on-task (office level), customer satisfaction (project level), and proofreading errors (activity level).

Establishing institutional accountability requires building a body of evidence. Evidence, in turn, takes on a variety of forms derived from a variety of data-gathering techniques. Rare indeed is the single technique that is sufficiently reliable, valid, and comprehensive to provide all the information needed for making an important decision. Thus, several techniques should be used in

ANCE INDICATORS TO GUIDE STRATEGIC DECISION MAKING

a triangulation process to furnish a sound basis for judgment. For example, although the Hayes–Lovrinic model yields important data about the relative costs of instruction delivered in seminars as opposed to large lecture sections, decision makers would want to look also at measures of student mastery of content and satisfaction with mode of instruction before making the decision to eliminate the more costly seminars from the instructional inventory. In addition to the traditional data-gathering techniques of paper-and-pencil tests and questionnaires, interviews, focus groups, and archival data such as student transcripts, we now have opportunities to track student behaviors electronically via analysis of such transactions as attempts to schedule a given course during registration or errors made in solving problems in a computer-adaptive test. In Chapter Two, Ewell and Jones describe some indirect measures of student learning that hold promise for directly increasing faculty behaviors that research has shown to be effective in promoting learning.

When the National Study Panel on Education Indicators was convened by the National Center on Education Statistics in 1989, some of the initial discussions of the panel revolved around whether or not to suggest the development of a mega-indicator of the state of health of the nation's education system that would be analogous to the often-quoted gross national product or the consumer price index. The mega-indicator might be conceived as a composite of several less comprehensive measures. No one on the panel was willing or able to describe such a composite, but the pyramid of information described above provides a foundation upon which to build one or more such indicators.

At Indiana University–Purdue University Indianapolis (IUPUI), we have a committed chancellor and the authors are attempting to provide the coordination for campuswide planning, assessment, and improvement. As Jongbloed and Westerheijden suggest, peer review is the most widely respected method of assessing quality in higher education worldwide. We have chosen to collect information on campus PIs in a conscientiously implemented program review process. Though not yet smoothly aligned, state accountability measures have been incorporated within the campus goals framework. Each department compiles a self-study based in part on such PIs as student enrollment, retention, and degree production over the past five years, which is supplied by the institutional research office; financial data supplied by the budget office; and a description of library resources contributed by the department's liaison with the University Library. A team composed of disciplinary peers, community representatives, and IUPUI colleagues from other units judges the extent to which a given department is contributing to the campus (and state) mission as it studies the department's presentation of PIs during its program review. A review follow-up procedure ensures that the department's performance is linked with the campus resource allocation process.

Using PIs in Decision Making. Performance indicators should inform decision making. Depending on the purpose for which they are developed, PIs should be used to provide evidence of accountability or direction for improvement, preferably both.

Perhaps the surest way to ensure that PIs will be used is to involve the individuals who ought to use them in their initial selection and development. Suppose that decision makers determine that a student satisfaction survey will enable them to convince state legislators to fund a new library or to convince librarians to devote more time to helping students use on-line reference tools. Such decision makers will be much more interested in the results of the survey than if they had not been involved in deciding what the indicators would be and how data would be gathered to define them.

The meaning of indicators should be clear and easily communicated. Summary reports tailored to various audiences should be prepared. In the example just cited, the student library use and need statistics extracted from the satisfaction survey for use by librarians probably would not be mentioned in the report prepared for legislators, although both were derived from the same instrument.

Providing indicator data from multiple sources will also help to ensure its use by decision makers. Adding data showing that faculty and community members share students' sense of need for a new library will be more convincing than the indicators of student need standing alone. Time-series data showing that these needs have increased over time are even more compelling, as are comparative statistics from peer institutions showing the availability of superior library resources on those campuses.

Bringing full-circle the argument for parsimony in developing indicator systems that will serve both accountability and improvement purposes, we might take as an example one of the most passionately debated questions confronting higher education today: Can faculty involvement in research be justified in terms of its contribution to undergraduate student learning? Both accountability and improvement purposes could be achieved if faculty could agree to pay attention to and increase the quality and quantity of such indicators as student perceptions of intellectual gain as a result of being involved with faculty in research, student opportunities to apply specified classroom learning while assisting in faculty research, and student opportunities to engage in collaborative learning with other students as all are engaged with faculty in research.

Choosing and Using Performance Indicators

The chapters of this volume, and many of the additional materials employed as references, provide guidance in two areas: how to choose appropriate performance indicators and how to use them. Ewell and Jones gave criteria for the choice of state-level PIs and also provided several examples from institutions and states on the effective use of PIs for accountability and improvement. Jongbloed and Westerheijden described how several European national governments have attempted to use PIs to rationalize funding decisions and experienced institutional backlash that has moved the focus away from resource allocation and toward quality assurance.

The authors of Chapters Four, Five, and Six of this volume turned their attention more toward the use of performance indicators. In Chapter Four, Dooris and Teeter describe the role of PIs in quality improvement processes with many examples from The Pennsylvania State University experience. In Chapter Five, Dolence and Norris describe a strategic planning methodology based on the initial articulation of key performance indicators and illustrate the implementation of this methodology at two very different institutions. Finally, DeHayes and Lovrinic explain in Chapter Six how indicators arising from an activity-based costing methodology have been used within the Indiana University system to help redesign the structure and processes for producing several important educational products.

Early in this chapter, we introduced five criteria for judging performance indicators. Two of these criteria—purpose and alignment across inputs, processes, and outcomes—speak more to the choice of PIs. The other three—coordination throughout the system, coordination of methods, and use in decision making—explicate usage issues.

However, the choice and usage issues cannot be separated. As both the European and United States experiences to date have shown, efforts to choose performance indicators without regard to how they can or will be used are doomed to failure. This lesson holds true as well for efforts to use performance indicators that have not been chosen carefully by those who must ultimately use the resulting information to improve program, institutional, or system performance.

Role of the Institutional Researcher

Everything said to this point leads to the conclusion that those who perform institutional research functions on behalf of a program, institution, or system cannot develop performance indicators by themselves. The institutional researcher's role in this process is that of facilitator or, as Borden and Delaney (1989) have suggested, an information broker who has "sufficient knowledge of the administrative issues confronting decision-making groups, an understanding of the decision-making processes among individuals and within groups and organizations, access and analysis of appropriate information in a timely and reliable fashion, and application of information to the process, so as to inform and improve decision making outcomes" (p. 50).

The institutional researcher's role is most obvious during the implementation of a performance indicator system when data must be assembled, analyzed, and reported. He or she can also play a crucial role in the development stage by providing sound guidance based on an understanding of the literature and knowledge gained from past professional experience.

Often, PI development efforts move too quickly to available data without sufficient thought about appropriate measures. Institutional researchers can help to avoid this leap by advising PI developers regarding the nuances and vagaries of the data in relation to the concepts being measured. Ultimately, the choice of performance indicators must derive in a coordinated fashion from

the experience of individuals throughout the ranks of organizational governance and management. At the point of testing and implementation, the institutional researcher's knowledge of harvesting institutional information systems,
survey research methods, and environmental scanning techniques to furnish
the necessary data is essential for deriving valid and reliable indicators of program performance.

References

Astin, A. W. *Assessment for Excellence: The Philosophy and Practice of Assessment and Evaluation in Higher Education.* New York: American Council on Education and Macmillan Publishing, 1991.

Banta, T. W. "Assessment as an Instrument of State Funding Policy." In T. W. Banta (ed.), *Implementing Outcomes Assessment: Promise and Perils.* New Directions for Institutional Research, no. 59. San Francisco: Jossey-Bass, 1988.

Banta, T. W. "Toward a Plan for Using National Assessment to Ensure Continuous Improvement of Higher Education." *The Journal of General Education,* 1993, 42 (1), 33–58.

Banta, T. W., and Associates. *Making a Difference: Outcomes of a Decade of Assessment in Higher Education.* San Francisco: Jossey-Bass, 1993.

Chickering, A. W., and Gamson, Z. "Seven Principles for Good Practice in Undergraduate Education." *Wingspread Journal,* 1987, 9 (2), 1–4.

Borden, V.M.H., and Delaney, E. L. "Information Support for Group Decision Making." In P. T. Ewell (ed.), *Enhancing Information Use in Decision Making.* New Directions for Institutional Research, no. 64. San Francisco: Jossey-Bass, 1989.

Ewell, P. T. *Winona State University: Indicators for Improving Undergraduate Instructional Quality* (draft). Boulder, Colo.: National Center for Higher Education Management Systems, 1990.

Ewell, P. T., and Jones, D. P. "Actions Matter: The Case for Indirect Measures in Assessing Higher Education's Progress on the National Education Goals." *The Journal of General Education,* 1993, 42 (2), 123–148.

Farmer, D. W. *Enhancing Student Learning: Emphasizing Essential Competencies in Academic Programs.* Wilkes-Barre, Penn.: King's College, 1988.

John Harris, personal communication, September 1992.

Jones, E. A. "The Public Response to National Education Goal 5.5." *Assessment Update,* 1993, 5 (6), 8–9.

Dorcus Kitchings, personal communication, November 1993.

Loacker, G., and Mentkowski, M. "Creating a Culture Where Assessment Improves Learning." In T. W. Banta (ed.), *Making a Difference: Outcomes of a Decade of Assessment in Higher Education.* San Francisco: Jossey-Bass, 1993.

McLaughlin, G. W., and Snyder, J. K. "Plan–Do–Check–Act and the Management of Institutional Research." *AIR Professional File 48.* Tallahassee, Fla.: Association for Institutional Research, Spring 1993.

Dennis Martin, personal communication, January 1994.

Richards, M. P., and Minkel, C. W. "Assessing the Quality of Higher Education through Comprehensive Program Review." In T. W. Banta (ed.), *Performance Funding in Higher Education: A Critical Analysis of Tennessee's Experience.* Boulder, Colo.: National Center for Higher Education Management Systems, 1986.

Shewhart, W. A. *Statistical Method from the Viewpoint of Quality Control.* Washington, D.C.: Graduate School of the Department of Agriculture, 1939.

Special Study Panel on Education Indicators for the National Center on Educational Statistics. *Education Counts: An Indicator System to Monitor the Nation's Educational Health.* Washington, D.C.: Department of Education, September 1991.

Task Force on Assessing the National Goal Relating to Postsecondary Education. *Report to the National Education Goals Panel.* Washington, D.C. July 1992, vol. 92–07.

Tennessee Higher Education Commission. *Performance Funding Handbook.* Nashville: Tennessee Higher Education Commission, 1992.

Williford, A. M., and Moden, G. O. "Using Assessment to Enhance Quality." In T. W. Banta (ed.), *Making a Difference: Outcomes of a Decade of Assessment in Higher Education.* San Francisco: Jossey-Bass, 1993.

TRUDY W. BANTA is vice chancellor for planning and institutional improvement and professor of higher education at Indiana University–Purdue University Indianapolis.

VICTOR M. H. BORDEN is director of information management and institutional research and assistant professor of psychology at Indiana University–Purdue University Indianapolis.

Appendix: Examples from the Literature

Karen V. Bottrill, Victor M. H. Borden

Table A.1 provides a list of measures that have been cited as examples of performance indicators. These examples have been culled from the books and articles listed as references given at the end of this table. For each of these indicators, we denote whether the reference is to inputs, processes, or outputs of higher education. The reader will note that these measures require a variety of different collection methods ranging from extraction from institutional records to surveys of students, faculty, or other constituencies, and peer review of programs.

When presented in a list format, these measures do not conform to the primary criteria for PIs stated in the final chapter of this volume; that is, they lack purpose. We provide them as examples from which one can draw after purposes have been specified.

Table A.1. Examples of Performance Indicators

Subject	Indicator	Input	Process	Output
Admissions	Number of applications by available position	X		
	Number of requests for information or preenrollment as opposed to number of actual enrollments	X		
	Acceptances as a percentage of applicants	X		
	Matriculants as a percentage of students accepted	X		

Table A.1. (*continued*)

Subject	Indicator	Input	Process	Output
Admissions (*cont.*)	Satisfaction with procedures for admission to institution	X		
	Recruitment of targeted high school graduates	X		
	Recruitment of targeted community college students	X		
	Out-of-state recruitment efforts and enrollment proportions	X		
Advising	Average faculty advising load		X	
	Average number of hours per week spent advising students		X	
Collaboration	Research project collaborations (undergraduate and graduate)		X	
	Undergraduate student involvement in faculty research and active learning	X		
	Percent of students reporting having visited faculty during office hours	X		
	Percent of faculty reporting involvement with a student club or organization	X		
	Involvement of senior faculty in undergraduate classes		X	
	Organization of coordinating programs among institutions		X	
	Participation in coordinating bodies		X	
	Exchange of tuition facilities (videotapes, courseware)		X	
Community Needs	Community members' judgments of college career preparation programs			X
	Number of outside groups using college facilities		X	
	Educational and cultural facilities for adults from the region	X		
	Cultural activities for outsiders: number, duration, participation		X	
	Recreational activities for outsiders: number, duration, participation		X	
	Commercial use of infrastructural facilities (laboratories, library)	X		
Completers	Preparedness for job or career			X
	Satisfaction levels of graduates			X
	Placement in work force			X
	Employer satisfaction			X
	Placement rate of graduates in the work force			X
	Destinations of graduates			X

Table A.1. (*continued*)

Subject	Indicator	Input	Process	Output
Completers (*cont.*)	Employer satisfaction with graduates			X
	Passing rate of graduates in licensure exams			X
	Average time lag between graduation and first job by field of study			X
	Average income of graduates after X-years by field of study			X
	Unemployed/graduates ratio by field of study			X
	Adequacy of the output graduate with regard to the labor market			X
Continuing Education	Amount of contract education	X		
	Quantity, quality, duration, participation of continuing educational activities		X	
	Sponsoring agency perceptions of adequacy of customized training programs			X
	Impact of continuing education courses, programs, and service on community			X
	Community awareness of continuing education and community service programs	X		
Curriculum	Effectiveness of procedures for revision of existing programs		X	
	Number and percent of eligible programs accredited or reaffirmed	X		
	Inclusion of cultural and ethnic perspectives in curricula		X	
	Inclusion of knowledge about countries other than the United States		X	
	Relevance of education in relation to professional activities years after graduation			X
	Scope of the curriculum		X	
	Agreement between aims of the curriculum and the institution		X	
	Percentage of courses requiring students to engage in independent research papers, projects, presentations, or similar exercises		X	
	Range of choice of major subjects	X		
	Scope of freedom-of-choice curriculum in relation to the volume of the compulsory curriculum		X	
	Student satisfaction with instruction, programs, services		X	
	Degree of innovation or degree of innovative orientation		X	
	Amount of time, means, and results of institutionalized activities toward educational innovation		X	
	Peer review of interdisciplinary programs		X	

Table A.1. (*continued*)

Subject	Indicator	Input	Process	Output
Curriculum (*cont.*)	Total number of enrollments by institution	X		
	Total number of enrollments by course	X		
	Geographical origin of students	X		
	Enrollment per section	X		
Entering Students	Entry qualifications of students	X		
	Educational and professional experience of students	X		
	Average SAT/ACT scores of entering students	X		
	Motives for enrollment in higher education	X		
Facilities	Use of facilities by departments		X	
	Amount of research and study space per student (graduate or undergraduate?)	X		
	Amount of software per student in the audiovisual center	X		
	Quality of teaching space used		X	
	Number of volumes or books per student in the library	X		
	Telecommunications and computing resources	X		
	Resources for scholarly and creative activity	X		
	Resources for research activity and quality of research output	X		
	Average square teaching space by faculty, department, institution	X		
	Teaching space/research space ratio	X		
Faculty	Faculty use of new technology for instruction		X	
	Teaching awards and recognition		X	
	FTE faculty	X		
	Percent minority faculty	X		
	Percent women faculty	X		
	Age distribution of faculty	X		
	Percent of total FTE employees who are faculty	X		
	Faculty salary and benefits	X		
	Peer institution comparison of faculty salary and benefits	X		
	Percent of full-time faculty who are tenured	X		
	Number of partially or fully endowed professorships	X		
	Number of Chairs of Excellence	X		
	Educational qualifications through teachers' training	X		
	Number of faculty with completed dissertations	X		

Table A.1. (*continued*)

Subject	Indicator	Input	Process	Output
Faculty (*cont.*)	Number of faculty research or development grants awarded yearly		X	
	International activities of faculty			X
	Books produced by staff each year			X
	Chapters in books per year			X
	Journal publications per year by type of journal (referred, peer reviewed)			X
	National, regional, and local papers presented			X
	Average number of conferences organized, attended			X
	Paid consultancy rate			X
	Percentage of time spent on research		X	
	Contributions to professional organizations			X
	Consultancies or advice to government and government authorities			X
	Consultancies to industry and private organizations			X
	Consultancies to community organizations			X
	Participation in editorial staff of books and journals			X
	Membership of scientific advisory committees, scientific society			X
	Number of research grants			X
Finances	Library support compared with that at peer institutions	X		
	Tuition costs compared to other costs	X		
	Percentage costs for housing		X	
	Percentage costs for equipment		X	
	Percentage costs for library, audio/visual centers		X	
	Budgeted versus real expenditure		X	
	Percentage expenditure on innovation projects		X	
	Ratio of total expenditure in relation to budget for innovation		X	
	Percentage of budget spent on continuing training		X	
	Analysis of the expenditure for educational goals, surveys of budgets by types of costs			X
	Overall revenue structure—where revenues come from, how reliable they have been, estimate future trends	X		
	Overall expenditure structure—where resources are spent, what expenditure trends are		X	
	Institutional grant aid as a percent of tuition and fee income	X		

Table A.1. (*continued*)

Subject	Indicator	Input	Process	Output
Finances (*cont.*)	Institutional comparisons of significant sources of revenue (tuition, state appropriations, private gifts, federal contracts)	X		
	Possible new sources of revenue identified	X		
	Tuition and fees per out-of-state undergraduate student	X		
	Academic activity cost per student		X	
	Expenditure on central administration		X	
	Expenditure on libraries		X	
	Library costs per student		X	
	Expenditure on computer services		X	
	Expenditure on premises		X	
	Expenditure on career services and student organizations		X	
	Tuition and fees per out-of-state undergraduate student	X		
	Cost–benefit analysis of specific course, program, or service	X		X
Financial Aid	Number of four-year need-based scholarship	X		
	Number and amount of merit-based scholarships	X		
	Number and amount of nonservice fellowships	X		
	Stipend levels and work loads for GTAs and GRAs	X		
Graduate Education	Numbers of fellowships and assistantship	X		
	Number of graduate programs	X		
	Student population per program	X		
	Graduate student/faculty ratio	X		
	Supported graduate students (paid from department accounts)/faculty ratio	X		
	Work load of teaching graduate student		X	
	Merit fellowships per graduate FTE	X		
	Graduate section per faculty FTE		X	
	Average graduate student compensation from all sources	X		
	GRE score	X		
	Reasons for incompletion			X
	Passed doctoral examination by field of study			X
Research	Number of summer grants awarded yearly		X	
	Number of staff available for research	X		
	Number of research assistantships	X		
	Number of postgraduates by faculty	X		
	Usefulness of research results for trade and industry			X

Table A.1. (*continued*)

Subject	Indicator	Input	Process	Output
Research (*cont.*)	Usefulness of research results for education			X
	Technological merits of research			X
	Scientific merits of research			X
	Social merit of research: contribution of social welfare			X
	Esteem on national and international levels			X
	Relevance, adequacy, accuracy of the research method			X
	Interdisciplinary research		X	
	Collaboration with institutes and research stations		X	
	Progress of research		X	
	Number of new inventions and developments as a result			X
	Annual making of an inventory/project planning	X		
	Regular analysis of the research program at faculty level		X	
	Number of current research projects		X	
	Competitiveness of the research program in regard to research programs of equal value		X	
	Staff supported from external research grants	X		
	Value of research grants	X		
	Existing research equipment by faculty	X		
	Percentage of research expenditure by institution		X	
	Research on behalf of government, companies, societies	X		
	Circulation of scientific results for the population			X
	Amount of contract research	X		
Service	Student levels of public service		X	
	Public service opportunities	X		
	Relations with external organizations		X	
	Articulation of continuing education and community service students to other college programs	X		
Special Populations	Programs and services for reentry and nontraditional students	X		
	Structure of student population by age	X		
	FTE enrollment by racial or ethnic origin	X		
	Distribution by gender	X		
	Numbers of nontraditional, transfer, and international students	X		
	Enrollment level of special populations	X		
	Success level of special populations			X
	Special population progress rates		X	

Table A.1. (*continued*)

Subject	Indicator	Input	Process	Output
Special Populations (*cont.*)	Commencing student gender ratio			X
	Support services for special needs students		X	
	Ability of continuing education programs, courses, and services to meet the needs of various groups in the community, including the young, old, different economic classes, and unemployed		X	
Staff	FTE administrators	X		
	Structure of the staff by age	X		
	Working days lost through illness		X	
	Academic staff/support staff ratio	X		
	Years of working experience outside present institution	X		
	Staff recruitment policy	X		
	Staff mobility		X	
	Student/staff ratio	X		
Student Progress	Time to degree completion		X	
	Student progress rates		X	
	Percentage of students changing major		X	
	Attendance per section		X	
	Number of degrees conferred; program completion rate			X
	Dropout motives		X	
	Number of students passing propaedeutic examination by field of study			X
	Passed tests by course		X	
	Goal achievement reported by students			X
	Attainment of skills identified as course and program objectives			X
	Average course load taken		X	
	Percentage of students reporting that they cut two or fewer classes		X	
Student Support	Number, duration, degree of participation in recreational activities for students and members of staff		X	
	Scope of services provided (compared to peers)		X	
	Graduates' satisfaction with academic and student support services			X
Student Transfer	Percentage of students who transfer out of the university			X
	Percent who transfer in	X		
	Transfer rates within university system		X	
	Before/after the transfer comparisons (GPA, satisfaction)		X	

Table A.1. *(continued)*

Subject	Indicator	Input	Process	Output
Student Transfer	Comparisons with nontransfer students at the same institution (progress rates, GPA, satisfaction, skill level, completion rates)		X	
	General education requirements for students who transfer		X	
	Student satisfaction with preparation for transfer		X	
	Major feeder and transfer institutions	X		
	Reasons for transferring		X	
	Graduates' and other former students' satisfaction with transfer preparation		X	
Teaching/ Learning	Percent of faculty reporting use of individualized or alternative forms of instruction		X	
	Percentage of students reporting that they were encouraged to ask questions in class when they did not understand something		X	
	Percentage of students reporting that the grading and evaluation process used by the instructor allowed them to actually demonstrate what they knew		X	
	Percent of students reporting not being significantly challenged by class material and assignments		X	
	Average number of graded assignments or exercises given per course		X	
	Percentage of courses requiring a graded assignment within the first two weeks of the term		X	
	Percentage of courses allowing or requiring multiple drafts, rewrites, or resubmissions of student work		X	
	Average turnaround time for submission of final course grades		X	
	Percentage of students reporting that they generally receive graded assignments back from instructors within one week		X	
	Clarity in description of course aims		X	
	Clarity of tests		X	
	Congruence between teaching and testing methods		X	
	Average class size by level		X	
	Percent of classes taught by full-time faculty		X	
	Percent of faculty reporting giving students credit for active class participation		X	
	Number of internships, practica, or other practice-oriented courses offered per student		X	

Table A.1. (*continued*)

Subject	Indicator	Input	Process	Output
Teaching/ Learning (*cont.*)	Number of independent study sections offered per student		X	
	Percentage of courses requiring students to use the library as a research resource		X	
	Percent of courses requiring students to speak in class		X	
	Average number of pages of writing required by course		X	
	Average number of pages of assigned reading required by course		X	
	Percentage of seniors graduating without writing a major research paper during their undergraduate career		X	
	Grade distributions by class		X	
	Withdrawal rate per section		X	
	Average grades per exam		X	
	Average final grades per section		X	
	Average amount of time spent studying for class or working on assignments		X	
	Percentage of students reporting having asked at least two or three questions in class during the term		X	
	Number of items checked out of the library by undergraduates		X	
	Number of library computer searches initiated by undergraduates		X	
	Number of pages copied at library copying machines per student		X	
	Percentage of courses with a clear attendance policy		X	
	Percentage of students reporting that instructor held review sessions in addition to class time		X	
	Percentage of available library study spaces occupied by students 5:00–9:00 p.m.		X	
	Percentage of students completing their first year without checking a book out of the library		X	
	Number of incompletes granted per student in a term		X	
	Percent of faculty reporting efforts to create group projects or learning communities		X	
	Percent of faculty using noncompetitive grading criteria		X	
	Percent of students reporting participation in group study		X	
	Percent of students reporting out-of-class discussions with fellow students		X	

Table A.1. (*continued*)

Subject	Indicator	Input	Process	Output
Teaching/ Learning (*cont.*)	Probability that a student will be enrolled in two or more classes with fifteen or fewer students		X	
	Percent of faculty reporting efforts to create group projects or learning communities in their classes		X	
	Percent of courses including team projects		X	
	Percent of graduating seniors reporting participation in group study	X		
	Percent of faculty reporting efforts to create group projects or learning communities		X	
	Percent of students reporting after-class conversations with faculty		X	
	Average number and distribution of classes of fifteen or fewer students experienced by a student in his or her undergraduate career		X	
	Percent of faculty reporting knowing the majority of students in their classes by name		X	

Resources

Three comprehensive contributions from the European literature, these volumes provide general concepts, specific case studies, and plentiful examples of specific performance indicators.

Cave, M., Hanney, S., and Kogan, M. *The Use of Performance Indicators in Higher Education: A Critical Analysis of Developing Practice* (2nd ed.). London: Jessica Kingsley, 1991.

Dochy, F.J.R.C., Segers, M.S.R., and Wijnen, W.H.F.W. (eds.). *Management Information and Performance Indicators in Higher Education: An International Issue.* The Netherlands: Van Gorcum, 1990.

Kells, H. R. (ed.). *The Development of Performance Indicators for Higher Education* (2nd ed.). Paris: Organisation for Economic Co-operation and Development, 1993.

The National Center for Higher Education Management Systems has produced many documents related to the topic of performance indicators (see Chapter Two). The following two references represent a campus-specific effort and a more general treatment of PIs based on the "Seven Principles for Good Practice in Undergraduate Education" developed under the auspices of AAHE and the Johnson Foundation.

National Center for Higher Education Management Systems. "Winona State University: Indicators for Improving Undergraduate Instructional Quality." Unpublished manuscript, January 1990.

National Center for Higher Education Management Systems. *A Preliminary Study of the Feasibility and Utility for National Policy of Instructional "Good Practice" Indicators in Undergraduate Education.* Boulder, Colo.: National Center for Higher Education Management Systems, 1993.

A series of volumes originated from the work of the Association of Governing Boards of Universities and Colleges. These volumes furnish indicators along with normative values established through surveys of a wide range of colleges and universities.

Frances, C., Huxel, G., Meyerson, J., and Park, D. *Strategic Decision Making: Key Questions and Indicators for Trustees.* Washington, D.C.: Association of Governing Boards of Universities and Colleges, 1987.

Taylor, B. E., Meyerson, J. W., and Massy, W. F. *Strategic Indicators for Higher Education: Improving Performance.* Princeton, N.J.: Peterson's Guides, 1993.

Taylor, B. E., Meyerson, J. W., Morrell, L. R., and Park D. G. Jr., *Strategic Analysis: Using Comparative Data to Understand Your Institution.* Washington, D.C.: Association of University Governing Boards and Colleges, 1991.

The following documents describe two national efforts to define core indicators for the community college sector.

American Association of Community Colleges. *Community Colleges: Core Indicators of Effectiveness,* A Report of the Community College Roundtable. AACC Special Reports no. 4. Washington, D.C., 1994.

Doucette, D., and Hughes, B. (eds.). *Assessing Institutional Effectiveness in Community Colleges.* Laguna Hills, Calif.: League for Innovation in the Community College, 1993.

Four examples of campus-based performance indicators follow. The first is from the University of Tennessee, Knoxville and the remaining three pertain to an ongoing program at the University of Miami in Florida.

Banta, T. W. *Possible Indicators of Program Effectiveness for the University of Tennessee.* Knoxville: University of Tennessee Center for Assessment, Research, and Development, 1991.

Sapp, M. M. "Setting Up a Key Success Indices Report: A How-To Manual." Paper presented at the 33rd Annual Forum of the Association for Institutional Research, Chicago, Ill., May 17, 1993.

Sapp, M. M., and Temares, M. L. "Being Competitive in Time: Key Success

Indices." Paper presented at the 31st Annual Forum of the Association for Institutional Research, San Francisco, Calif., May 27, 1991.

Sapp, M. M., and Temares, M. L. "A Monthly Checkup: Key Success Indices Track Health of the University of Miami." *NACUBO Business Officer,* March 1992, pp. 24–31.

KAREN V. BOTTRILL is research assistant in the office of information management and institutional research and a graduate student in the industrial/organization psychology program at Indiana University–Purdue University Indianapolis.

VICTOR M. H. BORDEN is director of information management and institutional research and assistant professor of psychology at Indiana University–Purdue University Indianapolis.

INDEX

Academic Audit Unit (United Kingdom), 46

Acherman, J. A., 41

Activity-based costing model, 82, 104; applications of, 87–92; elements of, 84; limitations of, 87; steps in building, 85; strategic planning and, 88; use of, at Indiana University, 82–84, 88–92, 100. *See also* Economic performance evaluation

American Council on Education (ACE), 5, 6

Anderson, C. J., 6

Association of Physical Plant Administrators of Colleges and Universities, 56

Association of Universities in the Netherlands, 41. *See also* Vereniging van Samenwerkende Nederlandse Universiteiten

Astin, A. W., 14, 16–17, 26, 100

Banta, T. W., 9, 97

Beatty, G., Jr., 81

Blume, S. S., 40

Borden, V.M.H., 99, 104

Bottrill, K. V., 99

Bowen, H. R., 28

Brinkman, P. T., 6, 81

Carter, N., 11, 14

Cave, M., 6, 10, 11, 13, 18

Center for Research and Development in Higher Education (CRDHE), 5

Chickering, A. W., 31–32, 101

Clark, B. R., 37, 42

Committee of Vice-Chancellors and Principals (CVCP) (United Kingdom), 43, 48

Continuous process improvement (CPI), 9; methodology of, 15. *See also* Process-oriented evaluation

Coopers and Lybrand, 8, 56

Cost performance indicators. *See* Economic performance evaluation

Council of National Academic Awards (CNAA) (United Kingdom), 46

Cuenin, S., 11

Davies, J. L., 12

Day, P., 14

DeHayes, Daniel W., 8, 81, 100

DeHayes–Lovrinic economic model, 101, 102, 104

Delaney, E. L., 104

Deming, W. E., 17, 95, 99

Department of Education and Science (United Kingdom), 42

Department for Quality Audit (DQA) (United Kingdom), 46

Descriptive statistics, 11

Dochy, F.J.R.C., 10, 13, 18

Dolence, Michael, 8, 101, 104

Dooris, M. J., 10, 100, 104

Dunn, J. A., Jr., 56

Economic model. *See* Activity-based costing model

Economic performance evaluation, 81–82, 92. *See also* Activity-based costing model; Resource allocation measures

Education Commission of the States (ECS), 28, 30

Ewell, Peter, 9, 28, 29, 30, 33, 96, 97, 98, 99, 101, 102, 103

Farmer, D. W., 98

Federal Statistical Bureau (Germany), 39

Frackmann, E., 13

Funding. *See* Resource allocation measures

Gamson, Z. F., 31–32, 101

Garcia, P., 47

Gourman, J., 6

Gourman Report, 6

Gray, R. F., 24

Hamlin, A., 56

Hanney, S., 6, 10, 11, 13, 18

Harris, J. W., 59, 99

Hetmeier, H. W., 39

Higher Education Funding Council for England, 43, 45–46

Higher Education Quality Council (United Kingdom), 46

121

Hoger Beroeps Onderwigs (HBO) (the Netherlands), 39
Hüfner, K., 38
Hungerford, C., 56

IBM, 59–60
Induced course load matrix, 24
Input-environment-outcomes model, 14, 26
Input-process-output model, 13–14; accountability and, 17; methodologies of performance indicators and, 16–17, 99, 100

Jones, Dennis P., 9, 25, 28, 29, 30, 33, 96–99, 102, 103
Jongbloed, Ben, 10, 97, 102, 103
Jordan, T. E., 7
Jowett, P., 18

Kaufman, R., 13, 14
Keller, George, 8, 61
Kells, H. R., 6, 10, 11, 12, 46
Key performance indicators, 64, 82, 104; PEST analysis and, 67; strategic decision engine and, 64–80. See also Performance indicators
Kitchings, D., 99
Klein, R., 11, 14
Kogan, M., 6, 10, 11, 13, 18

Laurillard, D.M., 13
Lawrence, B., 5
Lee, Y. S., 28
Lenning, O. T., 28
Leslie, L. L., 81
Loacker, G., 98
Lovrinic, Joseph, 8, 100, 104
Lozier, G. G., 10, 51

McLaughlin, G. W., 101
Management information, 11
Martin, D., 101
Mason, T. R., 7
Massy, W. F., 6, 7, 81
Mentkowski, M., 98
Meyerson, J. W., 6, 11
Micek, S. S., 28
Ministry of Education and Science (the Netherlands), 40, 42
Minkel, C. W., 99
Moden, G. O., 101
Mora, J.-G., 47

Morrell, L. R., 11

National Association for College and University Business Officers (NACUBO), 7, 55, 56
National Center for Higher Education Management Systems (NCHEMS), 7, 9, 23–24, 55, 82; applications of performance indicators by, 27–34; approach to management information of, 24–27; criteria for assessing performance indicators used by, 28; performance indicator systems designed by, 31–32; view of costs and benefits in performance indicators of, 25–26
National Center on Education Statistics, 102
National Collegiate Athletic Association (NCAA), 12
National Education Goals, 29
National Study Panel on Education Indicators, 102
Norris, Donald, 8, 63, 101, 104

Ohio Board of Regents, 29
Organization for Economic Cooperation and Development (OECD), 5, 10, 46

Park, D. G., Jr., 11
Parker, R., 33
Patterson, V. W., 5
Peer comparisons, 6–7, 102; total quality management and, 53–54. See also Quality assessment
The Pennsylvania State University (Penn State), TQM in strategic planning process at, 51–52, 57–59, 60, 61
Perez, J. J., 47
Performance indicators, 5–6; accountability and, 97–98, 102; activity-based costing model and, 88–92; contrasted to other types of measures, 11–12; criteria for judging, 96–103, 104; criticism of, 10, 13; definition of, 11–13, 37; development of, 18–19, 104; examples of, 107–117; goals and objectives, 18, 96–98; historical context of, 6–10; improvement and, 97, 102; in Western Europe, 37–48, 97; institutional researchers and, 104; methodologies of, 14–17; strategic decisions and, 63–80; total quality management and, 51–62; uses of, 18–19, 27–30, 47–48,

103–104. *See also* Key performance indicators; *specific types of indicators*

PEST (political, economic, sociological, and technological) analysis, 66–67, 68, 69, 70; key performance indicators and, 67

Peterson, M. W., 6

Pew Higher Education Research Program, 12

Planning-management-evaluation systems, 24, 25

Polytechnics and Colleges Funding Council (PCFC) (United Kingdom), 44–45

Prins, A.A.M, 40

Process-oriented evaluation, 9–10, 17. *See also* Continuous process improvement; Quality assessment; Total quality management

Quality assessment, 37, 47, 101; in Germany, 39; in the Netherlands, 41; in the United Kingdom, 45–46. *See also* Peer comparisons; Process-oriented evaluation

Resource allocation measures, 7–8, 81, 83, 93; in Germany, 38; in the Netherlands, 40–41; in the United Kingdom, 42–43; methodology of, 14–15; use of computers in, 7, 15. *See also* Economic performance evaluation

Resource Requirements Prediction Model (RRPM), 7, 24, 82

Responsibility center management (RCM), 82–83, 84

Richards, M. P., 99

Rodriguez, S., 47

Romney, L. C., 24

Roose, K. D., 6

Rothwell, M., 18

Science Council (Germany), 38–39

Segers, M.S.R., 10, 13, 18

Service, A. L., 28

Seymour, Dan, 52, 59

Sherr, L. A., 51, 61

Shewhart, W. A., 101

Shirley, Robert, 8

Silver, H., 46

Sizer, J., 42

Sizer, V., 14

Snyder, J. K., 101

Society for College and University Planning, 56

Spaapen, J. B., 40

Special Study Panel on Education Indicators, 100

State Policy and Collegiate Learning Project (SPCL), 30

Statistischer Bundesamt, 39

Strategic decision engine (SDE), 64–66, 101; steps in, 64–73; use of, at Illinois Benedictine College, 76–77, 101; use of, at University of Northern Colorado, 73–76, 101. *See also* Strategic decisions

Strategic decisions, 63–64; definition of, 63; key performance indicators and, 64–66. *See also* Strategic decision engine

Student outcomes assessment, 9, 96; methodology of, 16

Student-Right-to-Know Act, 12

SWOT (strengths, weaknesses, opportunities, and threats) evaluation, 54; key performance indicators and, 72

Taylor, B. E., 6, 11

Teeter, D. J., 10, 51, 61, 100, 104

Tennessee Higher Education Commission (THEC), 97

Total quality management (TQM), 51–62, 95, 101; academic processes and, 52–53, 57, 61; definition of, 51; IBM and, 59–60; methodology of, 15, 54; peer comparisons and, 53; vs. traditional uses of performance indicators, 53–56, 62; use of, at The Pennsylvania State University, 51–52, 57–59, 60, 61

Transformation process model. *See* Input-process-output model

Turk, F. J., 7, 82

Universities Funding Council (UFC) (United Kingdom), 43, 44

University Grants Committee (UGC) (United Kingdom), 42, 43

van Suyt, C.A.M., 40

van Vught, F. A., 41, 47

Vereniging van Samenwerkende Nederlandse Universiteiten (USNU), 41. *See also* Association of Universities in the Netherlands

Vroeijenstijn, A. I., 41

Weathersby, G., 5

Westerheijden, Don F., 10, 41, 47, 97,
    102, 103
Weldon, H. K., 24
West German Rectors' Conference, 38
Western Interstate Commission for Higher
    Education (WICHE), 5, 7
Whalen, E. L., 82
Wijnen, W.H.F.W., 10, 13, 18
Williford, A. M., 101
Winona State University, Minnesota, qual-
    ity assessment at, 101
Wissenschaftsrat, 38, 39

Zemsky, R., 7, 81

ORDERING INFORMATION

NEW DIRECTIONS FOR INSTITUTIONAL RESEARCH is a series of paperback books that provides planners and administrators in all types of academic institutions with guidelines in such areas as resource coordination, information analysis, program evaluation, and institutional management. Books in the series are published quarterly in spring, summer, fall, and winter and are available for purchase by subscription as well as by single copy.

SUBSCRIPTIONS for 1994 cost $47.00 for individuals (a savings of 25 percent over single-copy prices) and $62.00 for institutions, agencies, and libraries. Please do not send institutional checks for personal subscriptions. Standing orders are accepted.

SINGLE COPIES cost $15.95 when payment accompanies order. (California, New Jersey, New York, and Washington, D.C., residents please include appropriate sales tax.) Billed orders will be charged postage and handling.

DISCOUNTS FOR QUANTITY ORDERS are available. Please write to the address below for information.

ALL ORDERS must include either the name of an individual or an official purchase order number. Please submit your order as follows:
   Subscriptions: specify series and year subscription is to begin
   Single copies: include individual title code (such as IR78)

MAIL ALL ORDERS TO:
   Jossey-Bass Publishers
   350 Sansome Street
   San Francisco, California 94104-1342

FOR SUBSCRIPTION SALES OUTSIDE OF THE UNITED STATES, CONTACT:
   any international subscription agency or Jossey-Bass directly.

OTHER TITLES AVAILABLE IN THE
NEW DIRECTIONS FOR INSTITUTIONAL RESEARCH SERIES
Patrick T. Terenzini, Editor-in-Chief

IR 81 Studying Diversity in Higher Education, *Daryl G. Smith, Lisa E. Wolf, Thomas Levitan*

IR 80 Increasing Graduate Student Retention and Degree Attainment, *Leonard L. Baird*

IR 79 Managing with Scarce Resources, *William B. Simpson*

IR 78 Pursuit of Quality in Higher Education: Case Studies in Total Quality Management, *Deborah J. Teeter, G. Gregory Lozien*

IR77 Developing Executive Information Systems for Higher Education, *Robert H. Glover, Marsha V. Krotseng*

IR76 Developing Effective Policy Analysis in Higher Education, *Judith I. Gill, Laura Saunders*

IR75 Containing Costs and Improving Productivity in Higher Education, *Carol S. Hollins*

IR74 Monitoring and Assessing Intercollegiate Athletics, *Bruce I. Mallette, Richard D. Howard*

IR73 Ethics and Standards in Institutional Research, *Michael E. Schiltz*

IR72 Using Qualitative Methods in Institutional Research, *David M. Fetterman*

IR71 Total Quality Management in Higher Education, *Lawrence A. Sherr, Deborah J. Teeter*

IR70 Evaluating Student Recruitment and Retention Programs, *Don Hossler*

IR69 Using National Data Bases, *Charles S. Lenth*

IR68 Assessing Academic Climates and Cultures, *William G. Tierney*

IR67 Adapting Strategic Planning to Campus Realities, *Frank A. Schmidtlein, Toby H. Milton*

IR66 Organizing Effective Institutional Research Offices, *Jennifer B. Presley*

IR65 The Effect of Assessment on Minority Student Participation, *Michael T. Nettles*

IR64 Enhancing Information Use in Decision Making, *Peter T. Ewell*

IR63 Managing Faculty Resources, *G. Gregory Lozier, Michael J. Dooris*

IR62 Studying the Impact of Student Aid on Institutions, *Robert H. Fenske*

IR61 Planning and Managing Higher Education Facilities, *Harvey H. Kaiser*

IR60 Alumni Research: Methods and Applications, *Gerlinda S. Melchiori*

IR59 Implementing Outcomes Assessment: Promise and Perils, *Trudy W. Banta*

IR58 Applying Statistics in Institutional Research, *Bernard D. Yancey*

IR57 Improving Teaching and Learning Through Research, *Joan S. Stark, Lisa A. Mets*

IR56 Evaluating Administrative Services and Programs, *Jon F. Wergin, Larry A. Braskamp*

IR55 Managing Information in Higher Education, *E. Michael Staman*

IR54 Designing and Using Market Research, *Robert S. Lay, Jean J. Endo*

IR53 Conducting Interinstitutional Comparisons, *Paul T. Brinkman*

IR51 Enhancing the Management of Fund Raising, *John A. Dunn, Jr.*

IR50 Measuring Faculty Research Performance, *John W. Creswell*

IR49 Applying Decision Support Systems in Higher Education, *John Rohrbaugh, Anne Taylor McCartt*

IR47 Assessing Educational Outcomes, *Peter T. Ewell*

IR39 Applying Methods and Techniques of Futures Research, *James L. Morrison, William L. Renfro, Wayne I. Boucher*

IR37 Using Research for Strategic Planning, *Norman P. Uhl*

IR36 Studying Student Attrition, *Ernest T. Pascarella*

IR35 Information Technology: Innovations and Applications, *Bernard Sheehan*

IR34 Qualitative Methods for Institutional Research, *Eileen Kuhns, S. V. Martorana*

IR33   Effective Planned Change Strategies, *G. Melvin Hipps*
IR32   Increasing the Use of Institutional Research, *Jack Linquist*
IR31   Evaluation of Management and Planning Systems, *Nick L. Poulton*